SEMIN ~~AR STUDIES IN HISTORY~~

Gen

Poverty and Vagrancy in Tudor England

Second Edition

John Pound

Lecturer in Education
University of East Anglia

LONGMAN
London and New York

LONGMAN GROUP LIMITED
Longman House, Burnt Mill, Harlow, Essex CM20 2JE, UK
and Associated Companies throughout the World.

Published in the United States of America
by Longman Inc. New York

First pulished 1971
Second edition 1986
ISBN 0 582 35508 7
Set in 10/11pt Linotron Baskerville
Produced by Longman Group (F.E.) limited
Printed in Hong Kong

British Library Cataloguing in Publication Data

Pound, John
    Poverty and vagrancy in Tudor England. – 2nd ed. – (Seminar studies
    in history)
    1. Poor – Great Britain – History – 16th century
    2. Poor – Great Britain – History – 17th century
    I. Title   II. Series
    305.5′69′0941   HC260.P6

    ISBN 0–582–35508–7

Library of Congress Cataloging-in-Publication Data

Pound, John.
    Poverty and vagrancy in Tudor England.

    (Seminar studies in history)
    Bibliography: p.
    Includes index.
    1. Poor – Great Britain – History.   2. Poor laws – England –
History.   3. Tramps – England – History.
I. Title.   II. Series.
HC260.P6P68   1986   305.5′69′0942   85–19747
ISBN 0–582–35508–7

Contents

Contents

For Catherine and Richard

iv

Seminar Studies in History
Founding Editor: Patrick Richardson

Introduction

The Seminar Studies series was conceived by Patrick Richardson, whose experience of teaching history persuaded him of the need for something more substantial than a textbook chapter but less formidable than the specialised full-length academic work. He was also convinced that such studies, although limited in length, should provide an up-to-date and authoritative introduction to the topic under discussion as well as a selection of relevant documents and a comprehensive bibliography.

Patrick Richardson died in 1979, but by that time the Seminar Studies series was firmly established, and it continues to fulfil the role he intended for it. This book, like others in the series, is therefore a living tribute to a gifted and original teacher.

Note on the System of References:
A bold number in round brackets (**5**) in the text refers the reader to the corresponding entry in the Bibliography section at the end of the book. A bold number in square brackets, preceded by 'doc' [**doc. 6**] refers the reader to the corresponding item in the section of Documents, which follows the main text.

ROGER LOCKYER
General Editor

Preface

This book was originally published in 1971. In the intervening years a number of books and articles have appeared which deal directly, or indirectly, with the subject of poverty in the early modern period, and the bibliography, in consequence, has been almost doubled. Some additional material (numbered from **78** onwards) and changes in emphasis have been incorporated into the text, and the Norwich material, in particular, has been revised and extended in the light of my own more recent research. I have also included details of my own research into early modern Norfolk and Suffolk in an extended introduction.

I have taken this opportunity to dispense with my original preface, although I remain grateful to the people referred to therein. In particular, I wish to re-emphasise my debt to my grandmother, to whom this book was originally dedicated. My own children were not born when the book first appeared but they, in their turn, have stimulated and encouraged me in so many ways that it seems wholly appropriate that the second edition should be dedicated to them.

Introduction

Since this book was published specific work on poverty and vagrancy has been particularly concerned with analyses of the numbers and types of people roaming the roads of Tudor England, with suggestions that the level of absolute poverty was less high than was previously thought to be the case, and with further criticisms of the work of W. K. Jordan.

The writings of Drs Beier and Slack have cast considerable light on the problems of poverty and poor relief in Tudor and Stuart England and both have questioned the veracity of contemporary writers such as Thomas Harman, with his detailed descriptions of organised vagrant bands; and they have suggested that vagrants, of whatever kind, were almost invariably young, travelling alone, and seeking a job, rather than being involved in criminal activity (**113** to **116** and **136** to **137** *passim*). That most wanderers were seeking work and that some, at least, found it is beyond doubt. I am not convinced, however, that Harman can be dismissed quite so easily. There seems no good reason for a person of his social standing to have deliberately invented the types of vagrant he describes so graphically, nor the individuals which he lists for his own county. In any case, it seems to me that what is of most significance is not whether a person was indicted as a hooker or angler, an Abraham man or whatever, but whether he actually committed the type of offence described – and of that, there seems little doubt. Even allowing for the frustrating fact that crimes are not always clearly designated, Dr Cockburn has pointed out that 'it is difficult to dismiss lightly the mass of contemporary evidence associating vagrants with crime, and particularly with crimes against property. Acts of parliament, proclamations, legal writers and private correspondents all agreed that vagrants constituted a menace to public order which was both serious and, at least, for much of Elizabeth's reign, increasing' (**84**, p. 62). Vagrant crime tended to be opportunistic, with thefts of property, especially clothing, relatively commonplace, and it was not uncommon for vagrants to work in small groups, if not large gangs (**84**, pp. 63–5).

The fact that people were arrested as individuals is not, to my mind, an argument for stating that most of them invariably *travelled* in this way. Some vagrants may well have moved around in groups, of whatever size, but entered the towns individually or in twos or threes for the very good reason that to do otherwise would have courted probable, if not certain, punishment. On the other hand, as the Norwich census indicates, it was possible for families to enter a town unmolested, provided they appeared to be at least relatively respectable and capable of providing some support for themselves.

Where urban poverty is concerned, it has been common practice to link the absolutely poverty-stricken members of the community with the wage-earning classes immediately above them, and to suggest that between them they may have comprised anything between 60 and 75 per cent of a town's population. Emotive terms, such as 'grinding poverty', have been linked to these statistics to portray a situation of all-pervasive gloom. This is no longer satisfactory. In recent years, historians have become more and more aware that even the apparently desperately poor were sometimes better off than was previously thought possible. Charles Phythian-Adams, for example, in his recent study of Coventry, has emphasised that some of those given nil assessments in the 1522 military survey had resident domestic servants in their households, as did a few of the Norwich poor in 1570 (**97**, p. 132; **98**, p. 46). He considers that 20 per cent would be a realistic estimate of the true rate of poverty in the town, a figure broadly in line with that of the poor in Elizabethan Norwich (**97**, p. 134; **98**, p. 107).

My own work on the surviving assessments for Norfolk in 1522 (eleven Hundreds plus the town of Great Yarmouth), and for the Babergh Hundred of Suffolk in the same year, makes it equally clear that a proportion of those assessed on 20 shillings worth of goods (not wages in these rural areas) were freeholders in their own right. The Norfolk proportions varied from less than 2 per cent in West Flegg to 29 per cent in Great Yarmouth, 36 per cent in Brothercross, 37 in East Flegg, 38 in North Greenhoe and as high as 46 per cent in Gallow, the smaller holdings predominating in the western part of the county. In Babergh Hundred some 9 per cent of the £1 men were also landowners. Many others must also have been renting land. Whatever the proportion, its owners were clearly less vulnerable to economic vicissitudes than those relying solely on their goods at this level.

While the annual value of land obviously varied according to its quality and situation, it is suggested that land valued at £1 may have corresponded roughly to the medieval virgate of 30 acres. If this is so, a majority of the East Anglian landowners had holdings of 30 acres or less, supplemented, in some cases, by property rented from others. This is particularly clear where the Babergh husbandmen and yeomen are concerned, little more than half of whom were landowners but all of whom were men of some substance with goods worth £3 or more. What is equally clear is that the possession of small amounts of land is not, in itself, synonymous with poverty in the way recently suggested by Professor Hoskins's *use* of the material, however, which is particu-p. 32). His figures are faulty in any case, for he appears to have added together every individual name, irrespective of whether it appears on more than one occasion, as many do, or whether the people concerned were locals or non-resident landowners. It is Professor Hoskins' *use* of the material, however, which is particularly misleading. He has divorced individuals' landholdings from their goods, asserted that those without land (60 per cent according to him) were property-less and rented what shelter they had, and that of those with land some two-thirds (620 is his figure) had holdings worth £1 or less, 'probably nothing but cottagers and small house-holders'. This unfortunate misuse of the material has been further exacerbated by the Belgian historians, Lis and Soly, who allege that 87 per cent of the inhabitants of Babergh Hundred lived at, or below, the poverty line (**92**, p. 71).

The figures referred to above grossly distort the true picture. The 1522 return records 1985 people actually resident in the Hundred, some of whom had landholdings in more than one village or township. Of these, 352 were described as men of no substance, 394 were assessed on less than £2 worth of goods and a further 27 were assessed on small amounts of land but did not have their goods recorded. The three categories together comprise less than 40 per cent of the whole and, as indicated above, they include a small number of landowners in addition to those assessed on land alone.

It is the land question which is at issue here, and in my view it should not be used as an indicator of poverty, as Hoskins, Lis and Soly have done, but rather as a guideline to distinguish between those wholly, or largely, dependent upon their wages or goods, and those others who were in possession of land as well. In Babergh Hundred as a whole there were 600 resident landowners, most of whom owned land in their own villages, some of whom owned it elsewhere in the Hundred. For virtually all of them, their position in society can only be determined by linking their landholdings to their goods; Sir William Valdegrave of Bures, the largest lay land-owner, being unsual in providing no details of his moveables. The landholdings of all residents of all residents in Babergh are summarised in the table opposite. If a man had more than one holding, the collective value is given.

As it happens, the proportion of men owning land worth £1 or less *was* two-thirds (albeit 400 out of 600) but most of them were far from poverty-stricken, two out of three owning goods worth £3 or more, with the median value falling between £10 and £19.

If landownership divorced from the possession of goods can distort the true picture of individual wealth, the same applies to any discussion of clerical poverty which is based solely on the value of an individual's stipend. In a recent, well-argued, article dealing with clerical poverty in the early sixteenth century, Michael Zell has examined the position of the unbeneficed clergy from this point of view, stressing that those with stipends worth £5 6s. 8d. or less were on a par with the wage-earner, and concluding that 'the average country priest could not have been a person of high social status' (**143**).

The Military Survey of 1522, which provides the land details discussed, also provides details of clerical goods as well as the value of their benefices or stipends; and an analysis of these provides a vastly different picture to that portrayed above. In Norfolk, where the material survives for Great Yarmouth and eleven Hundreds in the north of the county, only 6 of 116 stipendiary clergy had no goods to their names, while some 80 per cent of them had move-ables worth £2 or more, for an overall median of £2 13s. 4d. Few historians would now regard men of this standing as being poor, except in the most relative of senses, and fully half of the Norfolk clergy had goods valued above this level. In Babergh Hundred in Suffolk, the twenty-six stipendiary clergy were marginally wealthier than this, with a median value to their goods of between £3 and £4. Twenty clergy of similar status in Rutland were rather poorer, with 45 per cent of them owning goods worth no more than £1. Overall, however, there seems little doubt that the parish clergy were distinctly less poor than an examination of their stipends alone might suggest and that these, added to their goods, would provide an additional bonus rather than the reverse.

Similar caution must be used when considering the men 'of no substance', for a number of them were subsequently assessed on goods when the subsidy was levied in 1524. About one in ten were definitely too poor to contribute and this figure of one tenth may

Landownership in Babergh related to value of goods

Land values	Land only					Value of goods in £s						Totals	%
		1	2	3–4	5–9	10–19	20–39	40–99	100–299	300–500	Above 500		
To 3s 4d	1		2	1	1	1	1					7	1.17
4s–6s 8d	14	16	34	13	16	19	3					115	19.17
7s–10s	6	10	27	13	17	17	20	1				111	18.50
11s–£1	1	6	13	10	21	21	11	4	1			88	14.67
£1	5		3	9	13	21	20	8				79	13.17
Above £1–£2	1	2	3	3	9	15	21	8	3			65	10.83
£2–£3	4	1	1		5	11	15	13	8	2		61	10.17
£3–£4				1	1	3	9	13	5			31	5.17
£5–£9					1	3	3	8	5	1		20	3.33
£10–£25						2	2	2	8	2		17	2.83
£26–£50							1	1		1		3	⎫
£51–£100	1											1	⎬ 1.00
£101–£150											1	1	⎪
£151–£200											1	1	⎭
Totals	33	35	83	50	83	113	106	58	31	6	2	600	
Percentages	5.50	5.83	13.83	8.33	13.83	19.83	17.67	9.67	5.17	1.00	0.33		

be as useful a working guide to absolute poverty in rural areas as 20 per cent would seem to be for urban dwellers. The proportion obviously varied according to the prevailing economic circumstances, but it seems absolutely clear that we must take much more note of gradations of poverty than hitherto, and not apply emotive terms such as 'grinding poverty' to all those who may legitimately be described as poor when compared to their more affluent neighbours. The Norwich census seems to recognise this when designating the local poor as either 'very poor', 'poor', or 'indifferent', those in the latter category being clearly more affluent, in a relative sense, than many of their neighbours.

None of this ignores the problems of the poor, nor of their permanent insecurity, but it does attempt to see the problem in perspective and to view it in a more realistic light.

Those who were in need were undoubtedly partly bolstered by charitable bequests, but historians have always been aware that the true value of these bequests was less significant than Professor Jordan implied. His most recent critics, notably Messrs Bittle, Lane and Hadwin, have made it absolutely clear that the so-called 'explosion of giving' was, in real terms, much less than this. The two former have argued that the contributions made a negligible impact. Hadwin, while less severe, has suggested that in terms of available income bequests kept ahead of the rising population, but did little more than this (**117, 118, 127** *passim*). On the other hand, there is increasing evidence that contributions from the rates were far higher than Jordan estimated, and these, combined with bequests, were normally sufficient to keep poverty within reasonable bounds. It took the famines of the 1590s to strain the system almost to breaking point, and to flood the roads with those numbers of young people which have been held to be characteristic of the Elizabethan period as a whole (**144**, p. 211; **115**).

Part One: The Background

1   The Causes of Poverty

'The most immediate and pressing concern of government . . . for something more than a century (1520–1640) was with the problem of vagrancy. There is no doubt whatever that vagabondage was widespread, that it was organised and that it imposed on rural and village communities burdens and dangers with which they could not cope' (**18**, p. 78). Thus, with some exaggeration, Professor Jordan describes a problem which, combined with the much larger one of poverty in general, led to the frequent denunciation of those allegedly responsible; to various experiments by the larger towns, most of which had only limited success; to governmental legislation which, initially almost entirely repressive, gradually evolved into the great Elizabethan poor laws of 1598 and 1601; and, finally, gave an impetus to that great outpouring of mercantile charity which, more than anything else, kept the problem within reasonable bounds.

Poverty and vagrancy were not, of course, peculiar to the sixteenth century, despite the frequent protests and intermittent government action during the period. Before the fifteenth century had run its course a number of factors, ranging from the social upheavals following the Black Death to the disruptions caused by the Wars of the Roses, had combined to produce a class of itinerant beggars. Many genuinely sought work which was not available in their own locality. Some married; others dispensed with this formality. Either way, their children grew up knowing no other way of life. By the beginning of the sixteenth century virtually every corner of England had its share of these professional beggars. They were particularly numerous in the region of the larger towns, and as the century progressed their ranks were swelled still further by a number of events, some of national, some of local importance.

Retainers and ex-servicemen

Many vagrants were relatively passive individuals, a nuisance to the people they begged from, but little more than this. There were exceptions, however, and the most dangerous of these were the vagrants that had been trained in arms. Very broadly speaking, they fall into two categories: those who were ex-retainers of the great noble households, and the increasing number who had been involved in warfare from the reign of Henry VIII onwards. Obviously only a proportion, possibly a small proportion, of such people would have resorted to vagrancy, even as a temporary measure. But they had been used to warfare, to an exciting, if dangerous, existence, and very probably to a higher standard of living than they would have experienced in civilian life. The prospect of returning to a humdrum existence as an artisan, with all its vagaries and uncertainties, possibly the prospect of returning to no job at all, must have persuaded many of the bolder among them to earn their living in an easier way.

The problem began with the ending of the Wars of the Roses and was accentuated by Henry VII's laws against livery and maintenance. The first Tudor was by no means entirely successful in his drive against the overmighty subjects, armed retainers being a feature of many seventeenth-century households, but the combination of Henry's zeal and their own mounting expenditure led many noblemen to adopt a policy of retrenchment. Redundant retainers were not easily absorbed into the local economy but, being the men they were, they did not accept the situation with good grace. As Sir Thomas More was to point out, 'in the mean season they that be thus destitute of service either starve for hunger, or manfully play the thieves' (**24**). Not many 'starved for hunger' if they could possibly avoid it.

Vagrants with this background became progressively more numerous as the century progressed, if only for the obvious reason that increasing warfare led in its turn to ever greater numbers of demobilised soldiers and sailors flooding the labour market. These men were, if anything, more dangerous than the retainers. According to Edward Hext, the Somerset J. P., they numbered up to three or four hundred to a shire and were constantly pillaging the local inhabitants [**doc. 7**]. They were so strong that the enforcers of law and order were afraid to oppose them. Scores of them thronged the streets of the larger towns – London, perhaps inevitably, being particularly affected. They were especially troublesome in the years following the Armada. Thus in the summer of 1589, after the abortive expedition to Portugal, the returning soldiers were landed on the south coast. They were allowed to keep their arms and uniforms on the assumption that they would sell them to make up the deficiencies in their pay. Large numbers of them drifted up to London and a band of some five hundred threatened to loot Bartholomew Fair. It took two thousand City militiamen to deal with the immediate problem, and a proclamation threatening all mariners, soldiers and masterless men with death, unless they obtained passports to return home within two days, before the matter was finally dealt with. Even then, it was six months before the panic died down (**20**, xvii–xviii).

In due course, special provision was made for such people. Provost-marshals were appointed to apprehend and punish them, and on occasion special tribunals were held to inquire into their complaints. It was finally ordered that, on discharge at the port towns, all soldiers should be given a sum of money for their homeward journey and a licence permitting them to travel unmolested, provided they followed a specified route and arrived within a definite time. This was supplemented in 1593 by an Act which made general provision for pensions, as well as authorising local magistrates to provide financial aid to those in need on the way home, but it was stipulated that any soldier caught begging would forfeit his pension as a matter of course. Sensing the opportunity for gain, many vagabonds pretended to be soldiers, ultimately causing such confusion that the authorities were ordered to question all such people; genuine cases were to be provided with assistance, while the frauds among them were to be punished (**2**, p. 71). As with most causes of poverty in the sixteenth century, the problem of the demobilised soldier was one which waxed and waned. Normally it could be contained without too much difficulty. When it coincided with dearth and general economic depression it was another story. It was then that a man as level-headed as Edward Hext could be so frightened by the existing situation that he could write to Burghley with a prophecy of virtual disaster, and in so doing give an impression of general disorder that can all too easily be applied to the country at large and to the sixteenth century as a whole [**doc. 7**].

The rising population

The steady rise in population, in contrast, was an issue which affected much of the country and which increased in intensity as the century progressed. The rise was not constant. The severe influenza epidemic of 1557–8 actually reduced the population, with estimates of decline varying from 5 per cent at the national level to as much as 20 per cent in specific areas. Population growth was similarly affected by severe outbreaks of plague (Norwich lost some 30 per cent of its citizens in 1579–80 and was hit almost as badly at the turn of the century) and, to some extent, by harvest failure and famine in the 1590s. The overall rise is undeniable, however, and in Elizabeth's reign alone the increase may have been as high as 35 per cent (**96**, pp. 36–7).

Unfortunately the rise in population was not matched by a corresponding rise in employment opportunities. The position obviously varied from area to area, but in most districts too many people were pursuing too few jobs. Ironically, the difficulties were accentuated by the increasing demands for agricultural produce from the towns. The opportunities for profit encouraged land-owners to undertake more intensive, more efficient farming, and in some cases, at least, increased efficiency led to surplus labour being summarily disposed of. Unless alternative occupations were avail-able locally – and this was seldom the case – a man had no alterna-tive but to seek employment elsewhere. The situation was made worse by the fact that as the century progressed more and more farm workers became dependent on wages as their sole form of income, and progressively fewer were guaranteed employment on their fathers' farms (**34**, p. 598).

The cloth industry

For those living in the cloth-producing districts of East Anglia, Yorkshire and the West Country, the problem was less acute. Steadily increasing demand from abroad provided work for thou-sands of men and, when necessary, for women and children as well. Norwich and its surrounding district thrived on the worsted industry. In Wiltshire, many families were wholly dependent on the cloth trade for their livelihood. Small towns as far apart as Totnes in Devon and Lavenham in Suffolk grew incredibly wealthy on the proceeds of the trade. As most of the people engaged in industrial activities of this sort also farmed on a small scale – and sometimes on a large one – there was much less fear of unemployment than in purely agricultural areas (**26**, p. 84).

The cloth industry was at the mercy of external events, however. A sudden bout of plague, an outbreak of war on the Continent, a series of bad harvests reducing a man's purchasing power, the great rivers temporarily blockaded: any or all of these could cause a sudden falling off in demand and set up a chain reaction resulting in wholesale unemployment for those least able to counteract it. The government realised the dangers and, where possible, insisted on merchants retaining their employees even when work was lacking. As Cecil was to point out, 'the people [that] depend uppon makyng of cloth ar worss condition to be quyetly governed than the husband men' (**56**, p. 166). Even so, riots could and did break out. At Lavenham in 1525, for example, the commotion was sufficiently serious for the Duke of Norfolk to have to quell it in person (**14**, p. 19).

Alternate booms and slumps were a feature of the first quarter of the sixteenth century, and even if a man could temporarily weather the storm there was no guarantee that his original job would again become available to him. The urban wage-earner was particularly vulnerable in this respect, and far more likely to have to resort to begging than his rural counterpart. Outside the towns, redundant textile workers might be able to find work on the land and a trade crisis could thus mean underemployment rather than unemployment for a family. However, in the 1590s places as far apart as Dedham in Essex and Kingswood in Wiltshire claimed to be largely dependent on the clothiers and found the poor rate a crushing burden (**102**, pp. 164–5).

Enclosures

Despite its vicissitudes, the cloth trade employed far more people than any other single occupation, with the possible exception of agriculture. Its very success, however, inevitably led more and more people to take an interest in it, and it was realised that far greater profits could be made from this source than from simple arable farming. It was confidently asserted that a man who enclosed his land and turned over his holding to sheep farming could expect a return half as great again as that derived from his previous pursuits.

Who will maintain husbandry which is the nurse of every county as long as sheep bring so great gain? Who will be at the cost to keep a dozen in his house to milk kine, make cheese, carry it to the market, when one poor soul may by keeping sheep get him a greater profit? Who will not be contented for to pull down houses of husbandry so that he may stuff his bags full of money? (**26**, p. 24)

According to contemporaries, far too many people were prepared to 'pull down houses of husbandry', and the conversion of arable land to pasture led to one of the most controversial issues of the whole sixteenth century. It was considered sufficiently important for parliamentary commissions to investigate the whole problem of enclosure in 1517, in 1548 and again in the early years of the seventeenth century. Writers as discerning as Sir Thomas More and John Hales were convinced that it was a great social evil and the cause of much distress. Bitter complaints were made of the depopulating activities of ruthless landlords who were so little concerned with the suffering of their tenants that they pulled down their houses around their ears and, on occasion, went so far as to depopulate whole villages. Deprived of their livelihood, many people had little alternative but to join the ranks of the itinerant vagabonds.

It must be said at once that such a picture is considerably overdrawn, and takes into account only part of the problem. Depopulation there certainly was, but the worst of it was already over by the accession of Henry VII in 1485. Many people did become vagabonds for the very good reason that there was no alternative local employment, but this is not to say that they permanently adopted that way of life. A number obtained jobs in other localities and, provided they did not become a strain on overtaxed local resources, the authorities concerned tended to turn a blind eye to such blatant evasion of their settlement laws. Not infrequently, the settlers occupied houses owned by the local aldermen. Even in the Midland counties which were worst affected – Bedfordshire, Leicestershire, Warwickshire, Berkshire, Northamptonshire and Oxfordshire – fewer than 3 per cent of the total area was enclosed (**26**, ch. 1 *passim*).

Nevertheless, when all factors have been taken into account, it remains true that a problem existed, and it would be over-cynical to dismiss it as of little or no importance. In Leicestershire alone one village in three was affected and far more than 3 per cent of the cultivable area of the Midlands as a whole was enclosed. In consequence, copyholders faced imminent or ultimate eviction. This class was particularly vulnerable. If they lived in the Midlands they were in the one major area where conversion of arable to pasture was still a paying proposition, the soil over much of the region being equally well adapted to both types of farming. Their vulnerability depended to a large extent on their particular type of holding. If a man possessed a sound title authorising him to pass on his holding to his heirs, and if his rent was fixed and his landlord was debarred from imposing an exorbitant entry fine on his successor, he was normally safe. Few people were as fortunate as this. Some held their property for a specified number of years, and could be easily evicted when the lease fell in. Others were safe enough themselves, their period of tenure covering the lives of themselves and their wives, and that of their immediate successor, but sooner or later their heirs faced either eviction or its virtual equivalent, the imposition of a prohibitive entry fine.

Such conditions caused very real hardship, but a word should perhaps be said for the 'villains of the piece', the squirearchy, who were responsible for between 60 and 70 per cent of the enclosure that took place. In a period of steadily rising prices, the copyholders with fixed rents could make increasing profits from their surplus produce. The landlords, in contrast, had to combat this price increase while their incomes remained virtually static. If they farmed their own demesne their difficulties were obviously diminished; if, in contrast, they relied solely, or primarily, on rents they could find themselves in trouble, even to the extent of falling into bankruptcy. It is hardly surprising that they sought compensation at the earliest possible moment, whether by raising rents or by converting their arable land to pasture and recouping themselves from the profits of sheep farming [**doc. 3**]. It should also be stressed that they were not the only enclosers. Many yeomen made substantial fortunes from the type of situation described. In due course, a number of them extended their holdings, usually by engrossing or joining together what had previously been two farms. Some eviction, with all its ensuing distress, inevitably followed. When the occasion arose, men of this class could be just as ruthless with their less fortunate neighbours as the worst of the surrounding gentry.

It follows that not all copyholders could be evicted at the same time. Their tenancies fell in at different periods and their heirs took over their property at widely differing intervals. They could, and on occasion did, have recourse to law if their rights were threatened. Even if the worst happened, many would have had some reserve funds to draw on, and vagrancy would not have been an immediate threat. The really vulnerable people were the wage-earners, who grew in number as the century progressed; the younger sons who had no patrimony to look forward to; the villagers who relied on the common land for the maintenance of their few animals. With no title at law to the lands that they used, they stood to lose their all when enclosure took place, and they were very hard pressed even if a wealthier man did no more than over-stock the commons. People in these categories were far more likely to become vagrants. Some of them moved to unenclosed villages where they settled as squatters on the waste land. In areas bordering Blackmore Forest and Chippenham, for example, 213 cottages were recorded in 1610, most of which had been erected in the previous twenty-five years. Three-quarters of them had no land attached, although forty-one were rent free (**102**, p. 163). People such as this were not welcome. In Shropshire, where 'cottages mushroomed on the wastes and commons' and where a place like Coalbrookdale was transformed from a rural backwater into one of the most densely populated parts of the country, the labourers were described as 'the scums and dregs of many countries [i.e. counties or areas] from where they have been driven' (**144**, p. 269).

The inevitability of the situation was accepted even at govern-ment level, however. The Poor Law of 1598 specifically sanctioned the expenditure of parish funds for the erection of cottages for these people, and subsequently such provision became part of the regular business of Quarter Sessions. The law was abused. As late as 1654 it was asserted that 'in all or most towns where the fields lie open and are used in common, there is a new brood of upstart intruders as inmates, and the inhabitants of unlawful cottages erected contrary unto law . . . Loyterers who will not usually be got to work unless they may have such excessive wages as they themselves desire' (**32**, p. 278).

Some went to the towns. If they were few in number they were fairly easily assimilated. If they were numerous they created serious problems. The authorities complained bitterly that they turned whole quarters into slums, that they spread disease through over-crowding and that they disorganised the labour market by crowding out the native artisans. If they obtained a job, they still had to tread very warily for fear of encroaching on the preserves of the guilds. Some defied the regulations. Others, seeking a legit-imate apprenticeship, were debarred by the imposition of a prohibi-tive entrance fee, especially if it was thought that they had a large family to look after which could become a civic responsibility in time of dearth.

It would be too easy, of course, to assume that enclosure was synonymous with all things bad. A number of small farmers, in particular, enclosed their land in order to increase their output.

This was invariably done by agreement with their neighbours, caused no problems, and was indeed roundly praised by contemporaries. In 1548 John Hales went out of his way to ensure that the commissioners, appointed to investigate the evils of enclosure, were aware of the distinction between the two types. The stimulus in this case was the rise of population. There were many areas of England where arable farming was infinitely more profitable than sheep farming, and this was particularly true in the area of the larger towns. Broadly speaking, the urban population of England rose throughout the sixteenth century. The increasing demand from the cities provided a considerable stimulus to the local farmers, and in the case of London a stimulus to farmers much further afield. As very little extra land was taken into cultivation, more intensive farming was necessary to extract the maximum possible yield, and contemporaries accepted that the best way to do this was to enclose the land concerned. Not all soil was suitable for this purpose. In addition, if one was catering for long-distance markets adequate transport facilities were an absolute prerequisite. This meant that such development was necessarily confined to coastal counties or to those with navigable rivers.

Accepting that enclosure of common land did contribute to the problem of poverty, at least to a limited extent, how serious was this contribution? Professor Jordan has estimated that not much more than 1200 square miles of agricultural land were enclosed in the whole of the period 1455 to 1637, and that this probably resulted in the dispossession and possible unemployment of no more than 35,000 families. By far the greater number of these cases occurred before the beginning of the Tudor period. Paradoxically, too, the boom in the woollen and cloth industries, which caused such distress in certain areas of the western Midlands, probably created more employment than unemployment in the country as a whole (**18**, p. 62).

Nevertheless, when all reservations have been made, it remains true that in the Midlands, at least, some thousands of agricultural workers suddenly became landless, rootless men, principally as the result of two very active periods of enclosure at the beginning and end of the sixteenth century. In Leicestershire alone, one-third of the 31,000 acres enclosed between 1485 and 1607 were dealt with in the first twenty-five years of the period, and almost one-half were fenced or hedged in in a similar period of time at the end (**26**, p. 32). The same story is broadly true of the other Midland counties. To the peasants most intimately affected, it appeared to be one widespread movement to enclose and convert the land to pasture, with rich farmers taking up more and more land but giving less employment than ever before. They can hardly be expected to have viewed the situation with equanimity (**68, 34**, ch. 4).

Inflation

Even if employment prospects were good, the wage-earner, in particular, was at the mercy of the price rise which continued almost unabated throughout the sixteenth century and beyond. Historians are divided as to the cause of this phenomenon. The most popular explanation is that it resulted from European imports of American silver, but this is only partly valid even for Spain, and is very misleading when applied to sixteenth-century England. It was only after 1545, with the discovery of the famous mine at Potosí in Peru, that silver imports to Spain reached a significantly high level, and this does nothing to explain why prices in England had doubled by mid-century. In particular, it fails to explain the five-fold increase in grain prices, and the fact that these rose faster than either industrial prices or wages. Monetary inflation emanating from Seville may have played a part in the price rise, but it was far from being the main factor (**26**, p. 117).

Where England is concerned, a major factor may well have been the great debasement of the 1540s, which resulted in the silver content of the coinage being reduced by more than two-thirds between 1543 and 1551, and which was at least partly responsible for the mid-century uprush of prices. The poor can only have been affected adversely by such a development. In the sixteenth century all wages fell markedly, if expressed in terms of purchasing power, and those of the unskilled labourer most of all. Even their nominal wages did not begin to rise until 1545, and in most cases they continued to lag well behind prices (**26**). Very few people in this category had land holdings to fall back on. If their already meagre earnings proved insufficient to purchase the necessities of life they had little alternative but to tighten their belts, and in cases of dire necessity they had to seek the charity of their neighbours or starve. When it is remembered that the middle years of the century saw four successive harvest failures, in addition to the rising prices, it is hardly surprising that it also saw a series of minor uprisings as well as the major disturbances in East Anglia and the West Country (**62**).

The steadily rising population, which has already been referred to, was probably an even more important factor than exchange depreciation in leading to a steady rise in prices, for it led to increasing pressure on limited resources that failed to grow as quickly. In the rural districts more and more people sought ever diminishing quantities of land. Family holdings had to be shared by a greater number of people, less fertile land was brought under the plough, and still agriculture could not expand enough either to raise its labour force or to increase its productivity proportionately to the rise in numbers. The rise in rents which occurred in many cases led to still further distress.

The problem was accentuated to an even greater extent by the link between exchange depreciation and the enclosure of common land, a link that contemporaries were not slow to notice. The fact that foreign merchants could now buy English cloth cheaper than before led to a boom in sales abroad, with a corresponding demand for ever greater quantities of the staple product. Those living in the textile areas of England could not fail to prosper, whether they were merchants or artisans, but the stimulus given to sheep rearing by the debasement of the coinage inevitably led to a further spate of enclosure and at least some distress of the type described above. It was not entirely a coincidence that exchange depreciation and a fresh inquiry into the evils of enclosure took place within the same decade, and the connection between the two was vividly pointed out in a letter to William Cecil in 1550.

> The fall of the exchange within thys iiii dayse hathe cawsyd and wyll cause to be boughte clothes at lvi li the packe wyche before wold not have byn bowghte for lii li the packe; so that yow may perseve that the exchange doth ingender dere clothe, and dere clothe doth engendar dere wolle, and dere wolle doth ingendar many scheppe, and many scheppe doth ingendar myche pastor and dere, and myche pastor ys the dekaye of tyllage, and owte of the dekaye of tyllage spryngethe ii evylls, skarsyte of korne and the pepull unwroghte, and consequently the darthe of all thynges. (**56**, p. 157)

The bad effects of enclosure could, nevertheless, be seen by all concerned and even, to a certain extent, anticipated as the century progressed, with the result that some precautions could be taken. Similarly, people had little alternative but to adjust themselves to rising costs as best they could, and in the second half of the century the poorest among them were given some assistance by the Elizabethan governments' insistence on compulsory contributions to poor relief. They were further aided by the increasing interest of the merchants and others in the plight of the really destitute.

Plague

If it was possible to anticipate distress of the kind described above, the same was not true of that perennial scourge, the plague, whether it was of the bubonic or pneumonic variety, and it invariably left poverty, as well as wholesale mortality, in its wake. From the time the Black Death entered England in 1348 until its final disappearance in 1666, the country was seldom free from this menace. On occasion it affected much of the kingdom: more frequently, it was selective. London would suffer, while Bristol was untouched. Norwich could be decimated, while York was unscathed. Urban areas tended to suffer more than rural, particularly when the expansion of population led to serious overcrowding. A mild outbreak could be 'ridden' without too much difficulty. Wholesale contagion, such as that which carried off at least a third of the population of Norwich between 1579 and 1580, was much more serious, and doubly so when the plague returned. For twenty-five years, between 1579 and 1603, the East Anglian city experienced a serious outbreak every five years. The first led to the deaths of some 6000 of its citizens. A further 3500 perished in the onslaughts of 1588 and 1593, and a similar number met their fate in the last year of Elizabeth's reign and the first of James I's (**74**, ch. iv). Although rarely as serious as this, the same tale could be told throughout the country, and sometimes, as in 1535 and 1563, plague actually followed harvest failure (**96**, p. 47).

The poor were always the chief sufferers. Frequently crowded together in closely packed tenements, with little opportunity to flee from the contagion, they were far more vulnerable than their richer fellows, and the pestilence, once begun, spread like wildfire. The death of a man meant the disappearance of the principal wage-earner. His wife, and those of his children who were old enough, continued to work until, or unless, they too were afflicted, but their meagre earnings could hardly compensate for such a loss. Even if death passed them by, a poor family was seldom completely unscathed. Their wealthier fellows fled in increasing numbers from the stricken area at the earliest opportunity, and the absence of an employer invariably meant the loss of a job. It also meant the disappearance of those who would normally be called upon to contribute to the poor rate, and unless those that remained were willing and able to shoulder the extra burden, the poor – or at least a proportion of them – were again the sufferers. The problem was accentuated by lack of contact between town and country. In normal circumstances a husbandman's surplus produce found a ready market in the neighbouring town, but few farmers were prepared to risk contagion to augment their earnings. Normal supplies were thus cut off, and, unless the authorities had been sufficiently farsighted to allow for such a contingency, plague and famine reigned hand in hand. The farmers themselves may have had no food problems – unless, of course, the epidemic coincided with a deficient harvest – but they had become accustomed to the extra income derived from a steadily increasing urban population, and the loss of markets must have affected them adversely. As was so often the case, a depression of this sort was of relatively short duration, but to the small farmer whose profits were marginal it would mean at best a tightening of the belt, and at worst very real distress.

In a ruthlessly practical sense, however, plague aided hard-pressed, and often impecunious, local authorities. If the ranks of the poor were decimated there were fewer vagrants to be dealt with, fewer destitute to draw on already depleted funds. This advantage, such as it was, was offset by the numbers that became temporarily or permanently unemployed as a result of the outbreak, but if both factors were weighed in the balance the city fathers seldom emerged the losers.

Harvest failures

To offset dearth in time of plague, and to counteract the possibility of harvest failure, an increasing number of enlightened authorities provided permanent corn stocks, the citizens being taxed for their upkeep. Both Norwich and Great Yarmouth augmented such a policy in 1557, for example (**62, 74**, p. 192). The wisdom of this policy was never more clearly illustrated than in time of famine, and, as Professor Hoskins has pointed out (**62**), bad harvests were relatively common, disastrous ones not infrequent. On average, there was a harvest failure every four years. Far more serious than the isolated cases were the occasions when the harvests were deficient or disastrous for two or three consecutive years, such as those of the middle years of the sixteenth century which led to mass starvation, those of 1586–8 which saw famine conditions in what is now called Cumbria, and, above all, the four successive bad harvests between 1594 and 1597 which led ultimately to widespread famine (**96**, p. 37).

These years meant, in effect, that a majority of the poorer people in the areas concerned were short of food and drink for that period of time, particularly as a deficient harvest invariably led to a rise in the price of other foodstuffs. The labouring classes, who numbered anything from half to two-thirds of the population, were particularly hard hit. Few were guaranteed, or desired, regular employment (**49**). They were at the mercy of the climate, the seasons, a falling off in demand, and a host of other factors; anything which meant that their meagre earnings would have to be stretched still further was bound to affect them adversely. Their position was made still more precarious by the fact that an increasing number of them were relying solely on wages as the century progressed. Many of these people – perhaps one-fifth in the cities, one-tenth in the rural districts – were on, or just below, the poverty line, and a similar number were barely above it (**60, 61, 66, 67**). Not surprisingly, food riots were far from uncommon and the government, both central and local, had to keep a constant watch on the corn market, permitting the export of grain here, forbidding it there, and generally ensuring the adequacy of supplies. Failure to do so could well have led to insurrection, and the disastrous famines of the 1590s provided at least the impetus for the great Elizabethan Poor Laws of 1598 and 1601.

The dissolution of the monasteries

All the factors mentioned above contributed to the problems of poverty and vagrancy to a greater or less extent. Sometimes they acted independently, sometimes together. On occasion, large areas of the country were affected, but it was much more common for distress to strike spasmodically, with different areas being affected at different times. What was common to all was the undoubted role they played in making the poor poorer, at least for a time, and in adding temporarily or permanently to the number of beggars roaming the roads of Tudor England.

In contrast to this, what evidence we have of the social results of the dissolution of the monasteries seems to suggest that their fall made relatively little difference to the numbers of either poor or vagrants. Nevertheless, most of the earlier writers on the topic were content to accept the fact that the dissolution brought in its wake poverty to untold thousands. In general terms, it was asserted that monks and nuns were reduced to beggary; that up to 80,000 of their dependants were forced on to an already overfull labour market; that the relatively lax abbots were replaced by grasping landlords who resorted to rack-renting, enclosure and, on occasion, the wholesale depopulation of villages; that monastic charity was no longer available and that the decay of hospitality, particularly in the north, deprived rich and poor alike of an accepted means of sustenance (**10**, p. 151).

This exceptionally black picture has been considerably modified by modern research (**40**, *passim*). Certainly, few of the monks and nuns would have had to resort to begging for a living. A majority of them were pensioned, including all the abbots, priors and prioresses from the small houses dissolved in 1536, all the occupants of those small houses which were allowed to survive until 1538 or 1539, and all the monks and nuns from the larger houses which surrendered from November 1537 onwards. The last group included those who in 1536 had chosen to transfer to such houses from the smaller ones which were suppressed. The pensions awarded varied from house to house, the richer the property the greater the abbot's annual pension. Examples vary from the £100 awarded to the abbot of Fountains to the £3 6s. 8d. granted to the prioress of Nunburnholme. A typical pension list for the larger abbeys is that of Selby, valued at £739, where the abbot got £100, the prior £8, five senior monks £6 each, six others £5 6s. 8d. each, nine junior monks £5 each, and two novices £2 13s. 4d. apiece. In contrast, at the small nunnery of Hampole the prioress got £10, the sub-prioress £3 6s. 8d., five senior nuns £2 13s. 4d., four others £2 6s. 8d. each, and eight juniors no more than £2 apiece. Excluding the abbot and the two novices at Selby, the average pension was almost £5 10s., while the average at Hampole, excluding the prioress, was exactly £2 6s. 8d. These local averages are very similar to the pensions awarded throughout the country as a whole.

The life of the average monk must have been a hard one if he relied on his pension alone, while that of the nun would have been almost purgatory. In 1538 the sum of £5 6s. 8d. was considered too small a stipend to attract a prospective curate; £5 was not much more than a subsistence allowance. The steady rise in prices itself meant that, with no cost of living bonus, the purchasing power of the pension would slowly wane away, and in addition the sum awarded was not that actually received. There were nearly always deductions to be made. Thus the Court of Augmentations' receiver or official claimed a fee of 4d. for every £1 of the pension and an additional 4d. for making out the necessary receipt form if the pensioner did not supply his own. In addition the amount of the current clerical subsidy, then standing at 2s. in the £1 on all pensions, was deducted. In consequence, in an average year a monk with a £5 pension received no more than £4 7s. 8d. (£5 minus 10s. subsidy, 1s. 8d. receiver's fee and 8d. for two half-yearly receipts), and in war years only £4 2s. 8d., a subsidy of 15s. being then deducted instead of the normal 10s. Only the poorer nuns had any general tax relief, those with a pension rate of £2 or less being exempted from paying the subsidy from 1545.

If additional taxation was not bad enough, there were also delays in the payment of the pensions, partly through negligence and partly through the financial embarrassment of the government. A nationwide survey in 1552–3 revealed the fact that many pensions were a year in arrears, some eighteen months and a few two years or more. Inevitably this caused great hardship if a pension was the only source of income, with the result that some monks sold their pension rights, preferring cash to the uncertainty of future payments.

The combination of taxation, fees and arrears made life very difficult for the ex-monks, particularly if they were aged and beyond work and lacked the support of relatives. But the fact that they had a pension did not prevent the majority of the ex-religious from seeking employment in the Church and they were aided by the fact that it was in the interest of the crown to support them in this respect. Their pensions were granted for life, or until such a time as they were granted a benefice by the king which was equal to, or in excess of, the amount they were receiving. Thus, every time an ex-monk was nominated to a living in the gift of the crown there was one less pension to pay, and it is hardly surprising to find the monks benefiting exceedingly from royal patronage. It was even more to the advantage of these people to find employment at the hand of a private patron, for they were then allowed to retain their pensions in addition to the stipend from their new post. Opportunities of this sort obviously varied. Some ex-monks obtained prompt employment, others had to wait years before they were able to supplement their livings in this way. Most fortunate of all were those whose abbeys were already cathedral churches, and who were retained on the staff of the new foundations. They were not all lucky, but in the ancient cathedral priories at least, they had an even chance of obtaining such employment.

Many of the ex-religious, particularly those who had been placed in monasteries at an early age with no real vocation for the life, had no desire to seek clerical appointments, but sought instead to earn a living in the purely secular sphere. In most cases we have no knowledge of their fate, but some prospered exceedingly, displaying talents more common to the merchant class than to the monastic. Perhaps the best known of these is one Thomas Pepper. His pension amounted to no more than £5, but at his death in 1553 his cash bequests alone amounted to more than £86, and he also made provision for the disposal of several leaseholds, including a valuable ironworks at Westwood.

The evidence at our disposal, then, suggests that few of the ex-monks who were pensioned lived in dire straits. The existence of some may have been spartan, but in normal circumstances they were hardly likely to become vagrants. The same is probably true of those monks who declined the opportunity of remaining in religion when the smaller monasteries were dissolved. A minimum of 1800 regular clergy accepted capacities (a dispensation which relieved them of their monastic vows and enabled them to embark on a fresh career) at that time and were given a small gratuity to help them on their way. They were not obliged to take this action and presumably had some alternative career in mind, possibly as a chantry or stipendiary priest, a clerk or a tutor in a private household. Some may have anticipated employment as clerks in administration or business. Few would have gone out into the world without some forethought. The same is broadly true of the friars, although they had no alternative but to accept capacities and a small gratuity. They had no opportunity to transfer to another house, and as they had always lived on charity it was assumed that they could continue to do so.

If most of the monks were in a relatively satisfactory position, the same could not be said for the nuns. The majority of them had pensions which were far too small to give them financial independence, and they had few obvious ways of supplementing their income. Marriage was one, and when clerical marriage was legalised in the reign of Edward VI some nuns, at least, took advantage of this. Such unions were short-lived, the Marian government insisting on their dissolution, and there is no way of knowing how many couples were re-united when Elizabeth became queen.

Some of the nuns had wealthy relatives to provide for them, some had small or, on occasion, large sums of money bequeathed to them which helped to eke out their pensions, but the fact that few ex-nuns left wills suggests that only a minority of them died with property worth bequeathing. The fate of most of the nuns is obscure. We know that at least half of them were still alive fourteen years after the dissolution, a fact attested by the returns of the Edwardian pension commissioners, but for nine out of ten we know no more than this. The ten per cent of whom we have evidence were moderately well-off; the majority, in contrast, probably lived at subsistence level and, on occasion, below it. If any of the ex-religious were reduced to beggary they were drawn from those in this category, but how often and in what proportion we shall probably never know.

Positive information is again lacking where the servants of the monks and nuns are concerned, but we are at least in a position to make certain generalisations which are unlikely to be too wide of the mark. It was never intended that these people should be ruthlessly disposed of; indeed, in Dr Woodward's words, 'it is ... difficult to think of any vested interest which the dissolution act did not do its best to protect' (**40**), but it was extremely difficult to make adequate provision for all of them. Their numbers were extensive, scores being employed by the largest establishments, while in the smaller houses the servants were almost as numerous as the religious themselves. For the agricultural workers among them, the position was not necessarily a bad one. The Dissolution Act attempted to provide for them by stipulating that all future occupants of the monastic houses, farmers renting their property from the crown, or purchasers of their sites and demesne lands, should 'maintain an honest continual house and household'. As the new owner invariably took over the monastic site and demesne as a going concern he would continue to require agricultural workers as a matter of course, and future employment prospects were reasonably bright. The same was not true of the domestic staff. Unless the new owner chose to live on the estate, their services would not be required. They were paid off, getting small gratuities in addition to any arrears of wages which might be owing to them, but their chances of re-employment were not good. In the larger abbeys, at least, they were generally dismissed with a quarter's wages in their hands which gave them the opportunity of seeking other employment without being under any immediate pressure; but they had to compete for jobs in an already overfull labour market and this may have led to some joining the vagrant bands, if only as a temporary measure.

Apart from their servants, some of the religious houses also maintained a number of annuitants and corrodians. For the former an agreement was entered into with the monks or nuns whereby, in return for a substantial cash payment, the annuitant was paid a fixed annual sum, usually for the remainder of his life. It was mutually advantageous, the monks having the benefit of the cash in hand while the annuitant was guaranteed financial independence. A corrody was similar to an annuity except that the original payment to the monks, and the subsequent services provided by them, were usually in kind rather than in cash. In return for a gift of livestock, corrodians were provided with permanent food and shelter in, or near, the abbey. The differences usually reflect the social background of the people involved. Annuitants were frequently men of means who sought a secure investment for their surplus capital. Corrodians were less wealthy people who wanted security for their old age when their own tasks became too much for them, but they were by no means lacking in substance. In 1518 John and Agnes Hudson purchased a corrody at the Yorkshire priory of Esholt with a gift of thirteen head of cattle, three calves, forty sheep, six wethers, thirty-four lambs and twenty shillings each.

Both annuities and corrodies were of obvious advantage to both parties, and were by no means the least of the social services provided by the monks and nuns in the days before the dissolution. Fortunately for the people concerned, the rights of the corrodians and annuitants were fully protected by the Dissolution Act, the one difference being that corrodians were henceforth paid in cash rather than kind.

It seems undeniable that the loss of monastic hospitality must have affected both rich and poor adversely, for, whatever their other shortcomings, the monks seem to have maintained this tradition well and there is no evidence of any general falling of standards in the early sixteenth century. Nevertheless, it must be conjectural how long the same state of affairs could have continued. In the period immediately after the dissolution there were bitter complaints about the lack of facilities for travellers, but the fault seems to have been the pressure of inflation rather than any lack of desire on the part of the people concerned. It affected all people of substance, and whereas in the past they had been as generous as the monks in entertaining the genuine wayfarer they had to become increasingly selective as the century wore on. The decay of hospitality was a general phenomenon and the fact that it seemed to stem from the dissolution is no more than coincidence.

The question of monastic charity is altogether more controversial. The care of the poor was a duty which fell on the religious orders as a matter of course. They had a general obligation to distribute all food which was left over after meals to the local paupers at the abbey gates; they were also expected to execute the terms of various wills, which again usually involved the provision of food and drink to prescribed numbers of paupers at stated festivals or in commemoration of certain anniversaries. Perhaps inevitably, the generosity of the monks varied from area to area. At St Benet's Holm, in Norfolk, there were bitter complaints in 1526 that the poor were suffering because the excessive number of dogs in the house were eating all the scraps and leaving nothing for the poor. Similar complaints were made at West Acre in the same county. In contrast, it was reported in 1519 that the paupers at Markby in Lincolnshire were not only well fed but were actually being invited into the canons' hall for their scraps, instead of being fed at the abbey gates.

The provision of food was a daily occurrence, and the numbers of poor affected obviously varied according to the size of the monastic establishment and the zeal of the inhabitants. In contrast, the terms of a benefactor's will were precise and it was expected that the charitable bequests would be faithfully executed. Even so, the proportion of monastic income consumed by these charities was very small. At its lowest, at Syon in Middlesex, it accounted for no more than 0.3 per cent of the monastic income. The proportion at St Werburg's in Chester was 1.3 per cent; that of Fountain's in Yorkshire 1.7 per cent. There were exceptions. St Peter's, Gloucester, consumed 6.6 per cent of its income in providing for the needs of the poor; Norwich Cathedral priory used 8.4 per cent of its funds for this purpose; and Great Malvern in Worcestershire as much as 11 per cent. Most generous of all was Whalley in Lancashire, where out of a total income of £551 as much as £122, or just over 22 per cent, was spent on poor relief. Some £41 of this was used to maintain twenty-four paupers, a further £62 or so was consumed by the weekly distribution of two quarters of grain, and the remainder provided doles at Christmas and on Maundy Thursday. Significant as it was, the generosity of these houses had an insufficient impact on the national average, which remained below 2.5 per cent.

Taken at their face value, these figures would suggest that monastic charity was of little consequence, and that the lot of the poor cannot have been radically affected one way or the other by the dissolution. But it must be remembered that the Valor Ecclesiasticus, which recorded such charities when assessing the monasteries for the new royal tax of the Tenth in 1535, was only concerned with the amount of obligatory charity, and made no allowance whatsoever for the generosity of the monks and nuns in other ways. Contemporary accounts of their generosity vary. Simon Fish, no friend of the monks, alleged that the charity of the religious was non-existent. In contrast, Robert Aske, the leader of the Pilgrimage of Grace (the Yorkshire rebellion which occurred in 1536 partly as a result of the dissolution of the monasteries), was convinced that in the north, at least, 'much of the relief of the commons was by succour of abbeys', and his testimony was supported by others [**doc. 5**]. Where the amount of recorded charity is large, it is obvious that the poor must have been affected adversely by the disappearance of the abbeys. Distress may have been general, particularly in the more isolated parts of the country, but the truth is that we are largely ignorant of the real extent of monastic charity, and are likely to remain so.

The monks may have been as hospitable as ever: in some areas they may have played a significant role in relieving the poor, but there seems little foundation in the old notion that they were somehow less rapacious landlords than their successors. Rising costs emanating from the general price rise caused the monks as well as the secular landlords to seek additional sources of income. They too were compelled to overhaul the management of their estates, to raise rents and to renew leases at much less favourable rates. As many of the larger abbeys employed numerous laymen as stewards, receivers and bailiffs, and as these administrators were invariably drawn from the neighbouring gentry and landowners, it is not surprising that their advice to their monastic employers should be coloured by their own experiences. Whether as a result of this advice, or by their own volition, there were occasions when the demands of the monks were extortionate. Thus John Alanbrigge, last abbot of Byland, demanded an admission fee equivalent to two years' rent instead of the customary three months' for the renewal of a tenant's lease. On occasion, the abbots resorted to eviction, and not always as the result of economic pressures. In one instance a monastic head wanted to give a holding to one of his own kinsmen and in consequence laid considerable pressure on the aged couple who were the existing tenants. The man, one Thomas Brown, was deaf, lame and blind, and his wife was almost driven out of her mind by the threats of the abbot concerned. Both were eventually evicted, and there seems to be no record of their subsequent fate. Evictions and the raising of rents were by no means uncommon, sometimes resulting from the initiative of abbots who enclosed their lands and set about improving their properties. This was not always done with malice aforethought, but simply to keep pace with the cost of living. Significantly, such action becomes increasingly common in the two decades preceding the dissolution.

To sum up, the people who were adversely affected by the dissolution of the monasteries were probably those monks who had to rely solely on their pensions, assuming that they were around the £5 level; the nuns, who invariably had smaller pensions still, who remained unmarried and were not otherwise employed; the domestic servants who may have found it difficult to obtain alternative employment; and the unknown number of poor who had come to rely on the monasteries for their charity. There may, for a time, have been pockets of considerable distress. The vagrant bands may well have contained some of the flotsam resulting from this unprecedented upheaval, but we shall never be in a position to measure such disturbance statistically. Over the country as a whole, the effects, as far as the poor were concerned, were probably minimal, and it seems safest to conclude with Dr Woodward that 'taken all in all, the social consequences of the dissolution would appear to have been marginal rather than revolutionary'.

All of the aspects considered above contributed to the problems of poverty and vagrancy, varying in extent from area to area and in importance from decade to decade. Collectively, they were sufficient to cause considerable concern to the successive Tudor governments, and in the uncertain condition of the times they created a situation which may well have been exaggerated out of all proportion, both by contemporary writers and by subsequent historians. It is time to consider the extent of the problem, and to estimate how serious it really was.

2   The Extent of the Problem

Poverty was rife in England throughout the whole of the sixteenth century and beyond. It has been estimated that between one-quarter and one-third of the population of most English towns were below the status of wage-earner, and at any moment their numbers were liable to be swelled by a slump in one of the major industries (**48, 60, 67**).

The poor

All categories of poor congregated in the urban areas: workers subjected to the vicissitudes of the cloth trade; men too poverty-stricken to take up apprenticeship and thus compelled to work under restrictive conditions; the survivors of dying occupations; men in new trades that had either failed or were yet to make their mark; itinerant poor, attracted, perhaps, by the misplaced generosity of the local merchants and disinclined to move on; displaced rural workers; former monastic servants; returning soldiers and sailors; a miscellaneous flotsam that at best maintained the existing situation and at worst made it so bad that even the most apathetic of local authorities were compelled to take action.

Above them were the more affluent wage-earners, comparable to the class deemed taxable by the government in the first half of the sixteenth century, but they were themselves in a precarious position. A bad harvest, a sudden trading depression, a period of ill-health, and all too soon a man could find himself in the company of his less well-off neighbours. Contemporaries were well aware of the position. A census taken at Sheffield in January 1616, for example, revealed the fact that out of a total of 2207 people almost one-third (725) were begging poor and a further 160, too poverty-stricken themselves to contribute to poor relief, were unable 'to abide the storme of one fortnights sickness but would be thereby driven to beggary' [**doc. 6**]. In virtually every English town of any size, the wage-earners made up some 40 per cent of the taxpayers in the 1520s. Combined with the really destitute, they totalled at least half and, in extreme cases, up to three-quarters of the population, and were a potentially dangerous element in society.

Apart from the aged and indigent, there were, broadly speaking, two categories of poor: a majority who were prepared to work if given the opportunity, and a minority determined to avoid it at all costs. The latter group contained a whole host of individuals, ranging from the professional beggar on the one hand to the thief and murderer on the other. These people have been well described by Professors Aydelotte and Judges (**2, 20**) and will be considered in more detail below. We know much less about the non-rogue element. What material there is is contained almost exclusively in the censuses of the poor, usually taken as a prelude to the reorganisation of a city's scheme for the relief of its destitute [**doc. 12**] (**36**). Very few of these survive. The most comprehensive by far is that undertaken by the Norwich authorities in 1570, when details of over 2300 men, women and children were recorded (**98**). Apart from information about areas of the city in which the poor were most prolific, which is mainly of local interest, the census provides us with details of the most prominent age groups, the average size of their families, the extent to which their children were educated, and an almost complete trade structure which clearly establishes the most decadent occupations in early Elizabethan Norwich.

Despite the precarious nature of their existence, a suprisingly large number of the local poor, both men and women, had survived into middle or old age, almost a quarter of the adult population being sixty or more. A few were described as past work – usually the very old or the severely handicapped – but the great majority followed some occupation or other. Even so, for many of them, parochial assistance was an absolute necessity. Without it hunger was a certainty; starvation a very real possibility.

The 500 or so men followed a variety of trades. The most numerous were the labourers and textile workers, the 120 men employed in each sphere accounting for some 47 per cent of the total work force. Most of the remainder were concerned with building and leather work (10 and 12 per cent) or with the clothing, food and drink and metal trades, each of which provided employment opportunities for some 5 per cent of the city's poor (**98**, p. 16). The residue earned their livings in occupations as varied as quarry picking and plumbing, gardening and embroidery; between them they were engaged in almost one hundred different trades (**98**, pp. 97–8).

Seven hundred and thirty-five of the 833 women had recorded

occupations and all but eleven of these were in employment at the time of the census. Some three-quarters of them were concerned with spinning of some sort, 348 of them specialising in white warp. About one in eight was occupied with knitting or mending garments while others earned money washing, weaving, teaching or selling food (**98**, p. 99). Many of them were widowed or deserted by their husbands and a surprisingly large number were in their eighties or nineties. Several of these were still capable of work, and some were married to men only half their age. Most of the younger women had children to care for, but, in contrast to their wealthier contemporaries, their families were not large. Whereas the Norwich merchants averaged almost five children per family, the poor had little more than two. There were some notable exceptions. No fewer than seventy-five households had four children or more. Of these, forty-five had four children, eighteen had five, six had six and three families each had seven and eight respectively (**98**, p. 18).

With their parents living at little above subsistence level it is not surprising to find the youngsters being sent to work at a very early age, often as young as five or six and, in extreme cases, even younger. Fully three-quarters of all the children aged between six and twenty were in some form of employment, many of them in the textile trades. Where the sex of a child is given, it seems that girls were more likely to be employed than boys, but as this information is provided in only 30 per cent of the recorded cases, such a suggestion must be tentative in the extreme (**98** *passim*). Nevertheless many families were prepared to sacrifice this additional income, small though it undoubtedly was, to send their children to school. Some went to what were merely industrial schools, to learn knitting, for example, while others were instructed in the rudiments of reading and writing. The numbers concerned were small, no more than seventy-seven children, or some 18 per cent of those aged between six and fifteen being affected, but it remains a fact of some significance that any form of education was attempted, and it is doubly interesting that the city authorities laid stress on this aspect when they reorganised their system of poor relief. Illiteracy among the poorer classes was far less prevalent than is generally believed.

Above the level of the absolutely poverty-stricken in the city were those who possessed sufficient goods to have them recorded in an inventory, albeit one whose total value was less than £10. Sixty per cent of these individuals lived in houses which had between three and five rooms; only one-quarter lived in those with two or less. A few of them had animals, such as cows, pigs, horses or chickens and occasionally their value made up a large part of an inventory. Thomas Plowman, for example, who died in 1584 worth £5 19s. 3d., had a cow worth £1 10s. 0d. and clothing worth 18s. 3d. Bedding was almost invariably the single most important item in such inventories, followed by personal clothing and – almost improbably – books. One in five of the Norwich poor, at this level, had books recorded among their possessions, a fact which may reflect the activities of the city fathers referred to above (**145**).

In times of stress a number of the poor undoubtedly resorted to begging. Indeed, if the disgruntled Norwich authorities are to be believed, this was their major occupation, the jobs they were supposed to be following being little more than a front for less creditable activities [**doc. 19**]. For all that, the professional beggars were by far the greatest problem. In the absence of positive statistical material, any attempt to calculate their numbers is fraught with difficulties. Estimates range from the 10,000 quoted by Harrison in 1577 (**2**, p. 4) to the 20,000 recently suggested by Professor Everitt (**34**, p. 406). In London in 1517 the deserving beggars were said to number 1000, 'so impotent, aged, feble or blynde that they be not able to gette their livynges by labour and worke and also be in such extreme povertie that they may not lyve but only by almes and charite of the people' (**72**, p. 289); by 1594 there were apparently twelve times as many (**2**, p. 4). The Norwich census already referred to recorded details of 525 males and 860 females above the age of 16, as well as 48 undefined adults. Children under that age numbered 926 (**98**, pp. 95–6). The figures for the capital city may well be reasonably accurate. The Norwich ones certainly are, for the census survives. The others are guesses, however well informed. What is certain is that in the eyes of contemporaries the numbers of vagrants were large and that they were both a burden and a threat to the commonweal.

It would be wrong, nevertheless, to assume that every person wandering the roads of Tudor England was, by definition, a rogue. Many genuinely sought work and, if fortunate enough to obtain it, remained in their new locality. Their position invariably remained a tenuous one and they seldom emerged from the ranks of the poor. A number of them had to accept charity, some had occasion to resort to begging, but most maintained themselves at subsistence level.

The census of the Norwich poor provides some indication of the movement and subsequent rehabilitation of this type of person. In the ten years preceding it, 138 families had added to the numbers of the city's poor, 90 of which had their places of origin appended. A majority of them had emigrated from the surrounding country districts, but 41 families had origins outside Norfolk. Of these, 21 came from relatively short distances (15 from Suffolk, 4 from Essex and 2 from Cambridgeshire); a dozen from the north (including 6 families from Yorkshire); 2 from London, and individual families from Hertfordshire, Northamptonshire, the West Country, Ireland and Wales. One individual was described as Scottish (**98** *passim*). Most were employed, or claimed to be employed, at the time of the census, some actually owning the houses they were living in.

In contrast to the situation in Kent, where the poor traveller almost invariably travelled alone, at least 30 per cent of the Norwich immigrants arrived as families, a fact clearly illustrated by the ages of their children. A majority of the others could have arrived as married couples, but as their children were born in Norwich they could equally have entered the city as single people. Relatively few of them were very young, i.e. 30 or less. Approximately one-third of the adult males (47) were aged between 31 and 40 while rather more than one-third (51) were older than this (**98**, *passim*). This contrasts markedly with the situation in Elizabethan London at the end of the sixteenth century where immigrants were essentially young and male, and with the similar situation in Crompton in Lancashire, although here some of the youngsters may have been local beggars (**113**, p. 10; **115**, p. 209). In the early seventeenth century the numbers of wandering children, in particular, increased considerably in Norwich and, apparently, in the south-east, and their numbers were also on the increase in certain areas of the midlands (**145**, **137**, p. 366; **129**, p. 42). While young apprentices had always flocked to the towns, it may be that the upsurge in the numbers of very poor children was a response to the exceptional conditions of the late 1590s and afterwards, rather than an Elizabethan phenomenon as such.

Seventy-one of the 500 or so men recorded in the census had attained their freedom at some time, while a further 41 had been apprenticed but had remained journeymen. Textile workers (53), building workers (19) and men employed in the leather (17) and clothing (14) industries formed the bulk of such people (**98**, *passim*). The remaining four-fifths were too poor to be even apprenticed but, at least, they were not subject to the rigorous laws of the various crafts or tied to one trade, and they could if necessary change their occupation at will. Some turned to labouring. Others, originally cordwainers, became watermen; cappers became pattern-makers and worsted-weavers lace·weavers. A few supplemented their incomes by working as porters at the various city gates. Significantly, very few were ejected by the Norwich authorities when they revised the city's poor law scheme, those that were being confined to the most recent arrivals and some of the prostitutes. Employment, however infrequent, and even if supplemented by occasional poor relief, was apparently enough to ensure a man's safety (**98**, *passim*).

The itinerant beggar who finally settled down, ostensibly to earn an honest living, was a phenomenon understood by the Tudor justice of the peace and his subordinates. His presence was accepted, and unless he became too great a burden on the rates he could be safely ignored. No such latitude was shown to those permanent wanderers, 'the wretched, wily, wandering vagabonds calling and naming themselves Egyptians' (**20**, xxiv). Probably first entering Britain at the beginning of the sixteenth century, the gypsies were misunderstood from the beginning. Despite the fact that many, possibly the majority of them, sought only to maintain themselves at a reasonable level, there was an air of mystery about them, heightened by their apparent dealings with the occult and their claims to see into the future. In an age when witches, fairies and the power of the evil eye were accepted by even the most educated of men, the dark-skinned strangers were regarded with the utmost suspicion. The authorities feared them to such an extent that country constables and churchwardens paid bribes to gypsy leaders with Romany names such as Hearn, Gray and Jackson in an attempt to get them to avoid the parish. The central government went further. In 1530 Parliament legislated against them with exceptional severity, those who remained in the country being ordered to suffer imprisonment and forfeiture of goods. Twenty-four years later a felon's death was substituted for imprisonment. As the century progressed, difficulties arose over those of the race that were born in England, and in 1562, in an attempt to overcome the problem, it was decreed that anyone consorting with them or imitating their speech and behaviour was to be apprehended as a felon. The drive was unsuccessful and the gypsy remains with us still, subjected even now to occasional persecution by local authorities.

When all reservations have been made, however, it remains true that there were a number of people who were undesirable by any standards. For the dishonest among them, a fair day's labour was anathema and they were determined to go to any lengths to avoid it.

Outside the towns people travelled either individually or in groups. The groups were seldom large, varying from two or three people to as many as sixteen, but in times of real distress they could swell to the forty or fifty reported by magistrates as discerning as Edward Hext in Somerset. Whatever their numbers, if they came to the towns they almost certainly broke up into smaller groups or entered the town singly. To do otherwise would have invited detection, with at the least the threat of a whipping and, for some, the ultimate penalty.

Despite recently expressed doubts, it is at least possible that some of the vagrant bands may have been organised in the way described below by Thomas Harman. Certainly people were arrested for the offences he referred to, even if his designations were seldom used (**84**, p. 313, note 92) At all events, according to Harman the bands were led by the so-called upright man, a beggar stronger and imbued with a greater sense of leadership than his fellows (**33**, pp. 408–11). It was he who directed operations, who took the lion's share of the loot and had the pick of the doxies or bawdy baskets as the women members of the band were known [**doc. 9**]. His followers were a diverse collection of rogues. Those that were literally called such in Elizabethan times feigned illness to obtain what they wanted [**doc. 8**]. Others, known as rufflers, begged from the strong and robbed the weak. There were men who obtained a tenuous living by pretending madness, and others who purported to be deaf and dumb for the same purpose (**33**, pp. 413–14). Some, ostensibly tinkers or pedlars, used their trade as a cloak for less commendable activities. Many had known no other way of life. The products of illicit unions between men and women of the same breed, they were known as wild rogues and in due course further perpetuated their kind. Occasionally they were joined by a more dangerous type. According to Bishop Gilbert Burnet, writing in 1681, wandering monks and friars 'did everywhere alienate the people's minds from the government, and persuaded them that things would never be well till they were again restored to their houses' (**2**, p. 54). Most prevalent in the middle years of the century, this kind of activity apparently continued until well into Elizabeth's reign.

Men such as this seldom starved. The Norwich authorities complained bitterly of beggars throwing away the food they had received in lieu of money [**doc. 19**]. Edward Hext, the Somerset J. P., quoted examples of the same sort laying up for days in the local inns, feasting on sheep and cattle they had stolen during the day. In the country districts they terrorised the villages through which they passed and were quite capable of affecting the course of justice. On one occasion, at least, a local magistrate was so terrified by the threats of a vagrant that he had his sentence of a whipping remitted and was apparently glad to pacify the fellow so easily. The most violent among them were invariably demobilised soldiers. Sometimes numbering as many as three or four hundred in a shire, they split up into smaller groups for their begging activities. The local authorities were often afraid to oppose them, saying that they were too strong, but even when action was planned the beggars usually knew of it in advance. Disguised as honest husbandmen, they attended the assizes, sessions, and assemblies of J. P.s, and passed on the requisite information to their fellows [**doc. 7**].

Forces of law

In any case, the local constables were notoriously unsuited for their task. Those that Burghley noted in 1586, who were gathered in groups looking for a man with a hooked nose, may well have been exceptional (**2**, p. 67), but in most cases their duties were beyond them. Judge has indicated the extent of their tasks. They had to

> see that the peace was kept; arrest rioters and those who 'go around offensively'; pursue wrong-doers; apprehend eavesdroppers, night-walkers and 'vagrom men' and put them in the village cage pending the magistrates' investigation; see that the watch was kept and that the petty officials of the parish were appointed; collect assessments and fines; and inflict minor punishments, such as flogging and branding if there was no one else to do it. (**20**, p. 521)

As the most arduous of these duties was that connected with the arrest and punishment of vagrants, it is not too surprising that this was also the least well executed.

The constable was not helped by the attitude of his so-called assistants. Felons not infrequently escaped from the stocks or were rescued by their fellows because there were no adequate watch-guards. Thieves were allowed to escape 'because the covetous and greedy parishioners would neither take the pains nor be at the charge to carry them to prison, if it be far off . . . . At the time of the hue and cry they say to the constable "God restore your loss. I have other business at this time".' A contemporary estimated that no more than one in five felons were actually committed to prison, most men being content to regain their goods and not bother with a trial [**doc. 7**].

With this attitude prevailing, some of the vagrants were able to prosper exceedingly. Nicholas Gennings, one of the better known of the Elizabethan rogues, collected more than fourteen shillings in one day's begging, a reasonable return at a time when the average daily wage of a labourer was little more than sixpence (**2**, pp. 33–4). In Norwich the takings of one Mother Arden exceeded £44, most of it in old groats collected over an uncertain period, and all the product of begging. Rather arbitrarily, the authorities confiscated most of it, leaving her 6s. 8d. for herself [**doc. 11**]. These two examples may be exceptional, but they help to explain why many men and women found the life on the roads so congenial.

From time to time the Privy Council became convinced that desperate remedies were required. On these occasions, the inadequate police system was reinforced by specially appointed officers, such as provost marshals, who were given extraordinary powers to deal with vagrants. Where necessary, they were empowered to hang them without going through the normal processes of law. At intervals, searches were organised, the watchmen being reinforced by bands of volunteers. In 1571 eighteen counties were affected by searches such as this, 125 people being employed in Shropshire alone. The numbers caught inevitably varied. In the spring of 1596 almost 200 vagrants were apprehended in the North Riding of Yorkshire. All were condemned to death, but on appeal were entrusted to one William Portington who was ordered to set out on a tour of England with the band. The journey was expected to last about seven months and it was assumed that Portington would deliver them to their place of origin. The results are not known, but it must be doubted if he had any success (**20**, p. xi). Even in normal circumstances there were some keen officials. William Fleetwood, Recorder of London between 1571 and 1591, for example, 'took an almost malicious delight in disturbing the quiet lives of the criminal orders and in hounding them off in great batches to Tyburn' (**20**, p. xxxviii).

Responsibility for this large collection of individuals, whether professional vagrant or poverty-stricken artisan, placed a heavy burden on the shoulders of local officials. They had to contend with two major interrelated problems, the preservation of law and order and the maintenance of the various categories of poor. Responsibility for these people, whether idle, infirm or momentarily unemployed, was accepted only reluctantly, and it was not until the end of the century that a satisfactory national system of poor relief was established.

Disorders

Keeping the poverty-stricken masses quiescent was another problem entirely, but that it should be accomplished more or less successfully was considered to be a prerequisite for the safety of the realm. Contemporaries were at once both contemptuous and fearful of the lower orders. While one person could comment that 'the poorer and meaner people . . . have no interest in the commonweal but the use of breath . . . and that no account is made of them, but only to be ruled'; another, more fearful, stressed that 'the multitude are always dangerous to the peace of the kingdom, and having nothing to lose willingly embrace all means of innovation, in the hope of gaining something by other men's ruin' (**59**, p. 301).

These fears were not unfounded. Protests over the granting of the subsidy for Henry VIII's French wars led to serious uprisings in Suffolk in 1525. A thousand men gathered on the county border at Stanstead in May of that year, those that were prepared to pay the tax were threatened, and the more timid among them went in fear of being 'hewn in pieces if they make any grant' (**14**, p. 19). A major uprising was averted on this occasion but 'more insurrection' was promised and occurred later in the year. A depression in the clothing industry in the area of Lavenham and Sudbury led to unemployment and caused considerable distress. Economic inequality was greater here than elsewhere, the wage-earners, who formed some 30 per cent of the population, owning less than 3 per cent of the personal property, and in a comparatively short time an 'army' of some 4000 men assembled. The locals must either have gained support from outside their immediate vicinity or been aided by their more affluent neighbours, for wage-earners and poor combined numbered fewer than 3000 men in the whole of the Babergh Hundred of Suffolk (**77**). In any event, the rising was sufficiently serious to warrant the personal intervention of the Dukes of Norfolk and Suffolk, and Wolsey himself had to order the clothiers to keep their men employed, irrespective of loss of orders (**70**, p. 257). The incident has been immortalised in Shakespeare's *Henry VIII*:

For upon these taxations,
The clothiers all, not able to maintain
The many to them 'longing, have put off
The spinsters, carders, fullers, weavers, who,
Unfit for other life, compelled by hunger
And lack of other means, in desperate manner
Daring the event to the teeth, are all in uproar,
And danger serves among them

(Act I, sc. 2)

There were minor uprisings in Norwich and Great Yarmouth in 1527 when there was a serious shortage of grain, and these were followed by the even more serious Ket's Rebellion, which broke out in Norfolk in 1549. The general details of this event are well known and will not bear repeating here. Sufficient to say that economic grievances played a major part in the disturbances, that the bulk of the participants were poor and that rebellion was the only way they knew of bringing their grievances to the attention of the government (**14**, pp. 70–1).

Minor riots were frequent, particularly in times of dearth. In 1596 the minute books of Newcastle Corporation record the deaths from starvation of thirty-two 'poor folk which died in the streets' (**28**, p. 399). The shortage of grain created a national problem in that year, but the people at large were not so quiescent as those of Newcastle. There were others 'that styck not to say boldlye they must not starve, they will not starve'. Edward Hext reported to Burghley that eighty such people got together on one occasion and took a whole cartload of cheese. The rich were blamed for the economic distress. It was said that they had everything in their hands and that they were prepared to starve the poor [**doc. 7**] (**59**, p. 303).

To a greater or lesser extent then, many of the very poor in Tudor England were living, at best, at subsistence level. At worst they slid below this, and then the more aggressive among them were liable to react violently, if only in a desperate attempt to prolong their existence. There was little sympathy for them. Before Elizabeth's reign the position of these people was tenuous in the extreme. The aged and impotent were permitted by the more enlightened towns to beg, although there was no compulsion to give them alms. The able-bodied were assumed to be unemployed by choice and were subjected to extremely harsh treatment, ranging from whipping and branding to mutilation and death. Following the experiments of certain towns, more humane methods prevailed in the second half of the century. First voluntarily, later under compulsion, parishes accepted responsibility for their own poor, but they interpreted this to the letter. Outsiders, if caught, were whipped and given passports authorising them to return to their place of origin. Occasionally specially deserving cases were given financial assistance. Thus in Norwich a couple were ordered to leave the town but were given half a crown to speed them on their way. Only the local poor were subsidised and they had to be absolutely destitute to receive such assistance. In practice help of this nature was given only to the aged, the infirm and the very young, and the numbers supported, if Norwich may be taken as a typical example, rarely exceeded 3 to 4 per cent of the existing population.

The problem

The methods adopted to deal with the various categories of poor will be considered more fully in the succeeding chapters. But how serious was the problem the authorities had to contend with? The foregoing would suggest that it was one of considerable dimensions, but one must be careful. It is all too easy for the historian looking back down the centuries to condemn the Tudor justice of the peace and his subordinates for failing to distinguish between the out-and-out rogue and the poor man who simply sought to earn a living. It would be equally easy to assume from contemporary accounts that the problem was far worse than it was. Rogues there certainly were, but a situation of the type described by Hext [**doc. 7**], or even a considerable increase in the number of beggars caught, often reflects intermittent depression or a momentary firmness as the aftermath of a major, or even local, uprising.

Fierce bursts of activity alternated with periods of almost complete indifference. Thus in the ten weeks between 6 October and 14 December 1590 seventy-one persons were sentenced to be whipped and branded at Middlesex sessions – an average of one a day (**2**, p. 71). In 1598 seventy-four people were sentenced to death in Devon alone (**28**, p. 392). Significantly, this was at a time when the harvests were extremely poor and when rioting and pillaging were liable to be far more prevalent than usual. In complete contrast, no more than twenty-nine beggars were apprehended in Norwich in 1570 and only twenty-six in 1571. It is true that these are figures for a single city, but after London that city was the largest and wealthiest in Tudor England (**77**).

The problem was never more than an intermittent one, even in the larger provincial towns, and was even less serious in the country districts. In the villages examined by F. G. Emmison in Bedford-shire and Essex, the income derived from the poor rate always exceeded the expenditure (**53, 54**). On occasion the surplus was sufficiently high to allow for repairs to the church fabric, to be invested, even on occasion to be embezzled; but there was always sufficient to maintain the genuine poor. If a person was seriously ill medical care was seldom lacking, and it was not unusual for a sick person to be provided with a joint of meat, with fuel and other necessities during the process of his cure. Sometimes the poor rate was collected intermittently, sometimes it was maintained over a period of several years, but there was always something to be drawn on in cases of emergency. In some areas it was the church or parish stock. A flock of sheep or a herd of cattle would be main-tained to yield an annual revenue for poor relief. St Mary's, Shrewsbury, for example, was letting out ten cows and three sheep in 1554, a move that produced £1 1s. 8d. a year for the parish. Charitably-minded persons made bequests with this end in view, no fewer than ten gifts of sheep being made to the village of Wootton, Hampshire, in 1559, making up a flock of twelve. Two cows left to the parish of Lapworth in Warwickshire were rented out at twenty pence a year, the proceeds being used for mending the road and relieving the poor. On occasion, the flocks could be quite large, Billericay in Essex maintaining forty sheep in 1599, all the proceeds going to the relief of the destitute. Parish flocks and herds of this sort continued well into the seventeenth century and were a valuable supplement to more normal methods of poor relief (**37**, pp. 9–10). Another expedient, until it ·clashed with Puritan ideals and was suppressed, was the provision of church ales. Carnival gatherings were arranged at which the corn provided was brewed into ale, the resulting profit being kept for the parish stock. Less frequently, a voluntary church rate was levied, the proceeds being used for church repairs and poor relief (**37**, pp. 11–12, 14–15).

Country districts, of course, had their itinerant vagrants as well as the towns, and there, as elsewhere, those with no passports were whipped and sent on their way. But there is nothing, in Mr Emmison's opinion, to suggest that either poverty or vagrancy was ever a serious problem in the areas he has investigated, at least until the disastrous harvests of the late 1590s, and Professor Jordan has pointed out that a total want of employment in rural areas remained almost unknown in sixteenth-century England (**18**, p. 67). Certainly, people were sometimes terrorised, and harvest deficiencies could cause serious problems leading to rioting and theft, but such incidents were normally few and far between. When they did occur the impetus was almost always simple hunger and the grim determination not to starve. It was the potential threat which caused most concern, both at national and local level, and it was this, above all, which led to the steady evolution of the Tudor schemes for the relief of the poor.

Part Two: Descriptive Analysis

3 Early Tudor Legislation

For almost fifty years those responsible for the government of Tudor England appeared little concerned with the dual issues of poverty and vagrancy. The only Act which dealt even remotely with the problem was passed as early as 1495. This stipulated that beggars and other idle persons should be placed in the stocks for three days, fed on bread and water, and subsequently whipped and returned to their place of origin. The Act was put into force rarely, if at all, and it took a severe economic depression in the late 1520s to jolt the government into further activity. Thousands of people became unemployed when diplomatic relations with the Low Countries were severed, and though the situation was kept under control by compelling the clothiers to maintain employment, it was far too dangerous to ignore.

The Act of 1531, which was a direct result of the depression, was the first attempt to deal adequately with the problem, in so far as it distinguished between the impotent poor and the able-bodied. No attempt was made by the state to accept responsibility for the former class, but they were at least allowed to beg officially, albeit only within their own community. No allowance whatsoever was made for the able-bodied man who was unemployed but genuinely wanted to work. It was assumed as a matter of course that employment was available for all who sought it, and the government acted accordingly [**doc. 14**]. Vagrants and unruly persons were to be whipped and returned to their homes. Any unlicensed poor who begged were to be fined, as were those rash enough to give them alms. Professional vagrants tended to ignore such stipulations. If they were caught they accepted their punishment stoically and proceeded to repeat the offence as soon as they were outside the authority of the justice concerned. The non-vagrant, but able poor were placed in an impossible position. Unable to find employment, yet forbidden by statute to beg, they had the alternative of breaking the law or facing death by slow starvation. Such men were literally driven into vagrancy. It is hardly surprising that they felt themselves persecuted by their superiors, and that on occasion they resorted to violence.

The authorities themselves soon realised the deficiencies of the Act, particularly the fact that no provision was made for the impotent poor, other than authorising them to beg. The whole problem of poverty was apparently thoroughly discussed again within a comparatively short while, and the draft of a further statute was drawn up in 1535 (**52**). It seems probable that it was prepared by William Marshall, a man close to Cromwell, and one who had recently translated and published the famous poor law ordinances of Ypres (1525–29). The draft recognised the fact that there was insufficient work available for all, and, in an attempt to rectify the matter, proposed an elaborate scheme of public works on roads, harbours, ports and rivers. Notice was to be given of jobs available, and all able-bodied unemployed were to report for work at reasonable wages, the alternative being arrest, forced labour and possible conviction for felony. It was to be financed by a form of income tax and contributions gathered in the parish churches. The impotent were to be maintained by public alms and their children were to be apprenticed. Specially appointed officers were to be responsible for any money collected.

The Act finally passed in 1536 completely ignored the scheme for public works, but it did order the parish or municipal authorities to assume full responsibility for the impotent poor to prevent them wandering around as beggars. Money for this purpose was to be raised by voluntary means in each parish, while casual alms were declared to be harmful and were carefully restricted. Any children of the poor were to be taught a trade and, in due course, set to work. Like its predecessor, the Act was at best partially succesful. The able-bodied continued to be lumped together in one general category, and it was still assumed that work was available for all who genuinely sought it.

Underlying all the Acts passed in this period was the fear of insurrection, and it was this spectre that continued to haunt the minds of Tudor magnates until well into the reign of Elizabeth. It was a fear that was particularly to the fore in 1547 when the nine-year-old Edward VI acceded to the throne. A lengthy minority inevitably meant the possibility of faction feuds, a possibility that became reality with the arbitrary seizure of power by the Earl of Hertford. Any increase in the size of the vagrant classes in such circumstances would be dangerous, and the members of the House of Commons proceeded to act with unexampled savagery. Under the terms of a statute passed in the first year of the reign, servitude for two years was prescribed for a first conviction, with penalties leading to lifelong slavery or a felon's death for the intractable (**50**).

Any man or woman who lacked means of support and remained unemployed for three days or more was deemed a vagrant as a matter of course. On conviction before two justices of the peace, the beggar was to be branded with a 'V' and then given over to the informant as his slave for a period of two years. In return for meals of bread and water, and the occasional luxury of 'refuse of meat', he was expected to perform any task his master gave him, however, vile it might be. If he refused, he was liable to be whipped, chained and, if necessary, imprisoned with iron rings round his neck and legs. The informant could capitalise on his property whenever he chose to do so either by selling the slave outright or by leasing him for a specified period of time. Should the master become ill, and look like expiring before the two-year period had elapsed, he was authorised to bequeath the slave to his heirs. Life was hardly likely to be congenial for the enslaved vagrants and it was assumed that some, at least, would attempt to escape. In consequence, it was stipulated that a runaway could be enslaved for life for a first offence and executed for a second.

In the event of nobody seeking the services of a convicted vagrant, it was ordered that he should be sent to his place of birth and there employed as a parish or corporate slave. The local authorities were given the same rights as an individual master. At their discretion, they could use the vagrant for parish work, lease him to individuals, or make an immediate profit by selling him to the highest bidder.

The large numbers of vagrant children posed a special problem. The authorities attempted to solve it in a way that would involve them in no extra cost and would at the same time provide the children with an opportunity in life they would not otherwise have had. It was stipulated that they could be seized by any person prepared to teach them a trade, the boys to be apprenticed until they were twenty-four years of age, the girls until they reached the age of twenty. There was no question of any premium being paid, nor was there necessarily any communication between master and parent. The Act specifically stated that such seizure could take place without the parents' permission, and if they attempted to reclaim their children they could find themselves enslaved as well. Slavery, perhaps, is not the most appropriate word to use where the children were concerned. It was obviously distressing to be separated from their mothers and fathers, but they were guaranteed regular meals and clothing, and if they showed any aptitude at all for their new trade they were given at least the possibility of secure employment in the future. They had little likelihood of such security in their existing environment. Nevertheless, runaway apprentices were not uncommon and the Act provided accordingly. In the event of a boy or girl fleeing from their master and being recaptured, it was decreed that they should be regarded as slaves for the remaining period of the apprenticeship. Presumably their working conditions would then be much less congenial, but their future would still be brighter than that of the average vagrant.

Although it allowed virtually no latitude for the able-bodied man, the statute was not entirely oppressive. It provided for impotent beggars to be sent to places of settlement, if possible, there to be provided for by organised charity. The funds for the purpose were to be obtained by a weekly collection in the churches, following 'a godlie and brief exhortacion'. Leprous and bedridden vagrants were to remain where they were, and appoint persons to beg for them by proxy. In the case of the able-bodied, provision was made for the discharge of any slave who acquired a 'convenient living', whether by inheritance or otherwise. This was less optimistic than it sounds. Edward Hext, in his letter to the Privy Council in 1596, made reference to a vagrant who was heir to land worth £40 [**doc. 7**], and it seems quite probable that there was always a sprinkling of such prodigals among the vagabond bands [**doc. 10**].

Despite these sops to tender consciences, the Act was more than local authorities could stomach. The parish constable was quite prepared to beat the really recalcitrant beggar and send him on his way, but to condemn a man to slavery for life was another thing entirely. There was nothing unusual about this. The Act of 1536 had threatened constables with a fine of five marks for refusing to mutilate beggars and two days in the stocks for neglecting to whip children. Sixty years later Hext was complaining that thieves were not being punished for theft because 'the simple countryman and woman . . . are of opynyon that they wold not procure a mans death for all the goods yn the world' [**doc. 7**]. With such an attitude prevailing, the ferocity of the statute made it a virtual dead letter from the outset. In 1550 it was repealed and the Act of 1531 was revived in its stead, little being salvaged apart from a section allowing the compulsory employment of poor children.

The middle years of the century saw two further Acts. In 1552, in an attempt to provide funds for the impotent poor, weekly collections were imposed, and it was stipulated that the amounts people were willing to pay should be recorded, an important step in itself towards a permanent poor rate. Those unwilling to contribute were to be persuaded, first by the parson and then, if he was unsuccessful, by the bishop himself. Persuasion was one thing, compulsion another, and until this was introduced any legislation was liable to be of limited use. The Marian parliaments were unwilling to go the whole way in this direction and a new Act passed at the end of 1555 included clauses authorising begging where the poor were too numerous to be relieved, and provided for richer parishes to assist their poorer neighbours with any surplus funds (**139**, p. 103) Both clauses were still being operated to the letter in Norfolk at the end of the sixteenth century, despite the introduction of a compulsory poor rate, which was to be one of the particular contributions of Elizabeth's reign (**120** and **123**).

4 The Elizabethan Poor Laws

When Elizabeth came to the throne in 1558 the parliamentary attitude to poor relief had changed little since the days of her father. It was still assumed that there were only two categories of vagrant, those who begged because they were incapacitated in some way and those who did so because they found the life congenial. The main Act governing the country's actions remained that of 1531, supplemented in certain particulars by the laws passed during the reigns of Edward VI and Mary I. It distinguished between the able-bodied vagrant, who was to be whipped, and the impotent beggar who was to be relieved, but made no provision whatsoever for the man who desperately desired to be employed but had no job to go to. A move had been made in the direction of parish responsibility for the poor, for whereas the laws of Henry VIII presupposed that they would be relieved by voluntary alms, those of his son and eldest daughter at least prescribed persuasion. This was clearly insufficient, however, and the laws in the mid-sixteenth century did little to deter vagrants or to relieve the poor.

The governmental mind continued to be haunted by the fear of insurrection. The uprisings and other troubles in 1548 and 1549 had produced no fewer than ten public proclamations against tale-bearers and spreaders of seditious rumours, all of whom were classed as rogues and vagabonds; and the next decade saw a whole series of letters directed to shire officers commanding them to do their utmost to suppress such people. In April 1551 directions for watches and punishments were sent to all the justices of the peace, and these were followed at intervals by instructions to the law officers of individual counties. In November 1552 it was the turn of Buckinghamshire; in September 1554 that of the Lord Mayor of London. The Norfolk justices of the peace were written to in March 1555; the lords lieutenant of Sussex and Surrey in 1559 and the Archbishop of York in 1561. A decade of intermittent activity culminated in July 1562 when letters were sent to the sheriffs and justices of the peace of Southampton, Devon, Cornwall, Hereford, Stafford, Chester, Berkshire, Buckinghamshire and Oxfordshire, and to Lord Rutland, Lord President of the Council of the North (**2**, p. 64).

Early legislation

It was at this juncture that the government took its first positive steps in the direction of a compulsory rate for the relief of the poor. London, Norwich and Ipswich had already taken this action, and once it was seen to be successful the central authorities tentatively followed suit in 1563. It was still hoped that the combined efforts of the parson and bishop would be sufficient to persuade people to support the destitute in their own parishes, but, if they were not, recalcitrant individuals were to be bound over to appear before the justices of the peace at the next Quarter Sessions. Continued refusal would lead to imprisonment until a contribution was made. No attempt was made to stipulate a specific sum of money, and presumably donations could be as small as the individual cared to make them.

In the same year the important Statute of Artificers became law. It had been preceded by attempts, at both local and national level, to control wages. Government policy was inconsistent in this respect. In the north it attempted, with limited success, to keep wages at the 1514 level. In the midlands and south, in contrast, it was prepared to be more flexible and allowed locally established rates to carry the day. Both local and central government were united, however, in the need to control the labour market and to set an absolute ceiling to wage settlements. Similar activity was evident where apprenticeship regulations were concerned. Many towns felt that too rigid a property qualification for parents of prospective apprentices would restrict the flow from rural areas, and Bills to gain exemption from such qualifications were re-introduced when the Statute of Artificers became law, London and Norwich being exempted as hitherto. The parental qualification was raised to one of £3 of freehold land per annum for those apprenticing their sons in market towns, but for those seeking apprenticeships with merchants, mercers, drapers, goldsmiths, ironmongers, embroiderers and clothiers in the corporate towns the qualification was set at £2. The variation suggests that the government, although clinging to its principle, was forced to make some concessions, especially to the larger towns (**142**, pp. 35, 37, 41–2)

The Statute dealt in particular with the occupation a man could follow, the training he had to undergo, and the wages he could be paid. Unless they came within certain well-defined categories, all males between the ages of twelve and sixty were expected to become agricultural labourers, a provision which would, theoretically, account for all the able-bodied unemployed. Those eligible for employment in one of the numerous industrial crafts were ordered to serve a seven-year apprenticeship, whether they lived in town or country. This was hardly an innovation for the urban areas, none of the Norwich apprentices, for example, ever serving less than the prescribed period, while many remained bound to a master for periods of eight, nine and, in extreme cases, ten years (**77**). The main objective was obviously to maintain high standards of craftsmanship and to confine industrial activity to the guild system. In theory, such a stipulation should have tied a man permanently to one trade, for few would wish to serve a second seven-year period. In practice little obstacle was placed in the way of a person genuinely wishing to change his occupation, provided he had the capital to do so. He was specifically debarred from ever practising his first trade again, but the initial move was relatively easy (**74**, p. 11). It was obvious, too, from the apprentices taken, that a master craftsman frequently widened his activities considerably as the years passed (**77**), and equally obvious from the evidence of inventories that a man's stated occupation, particularly in the country districts, often bore little resemblance to the trade that he actually practised (**63**, pp. 76–109). The enforcement of apprenticeship itself was apparently neglected by both local and central authorities, although wages were assessed much more frequently than was at one time thought to be the case (**93**, Introduction).

Both Acts, nevertheless, reflected the continuing anxiety of the government over the whole question of vagrancy and poor relief, an anxiety that found expression in the frequent directives of the Privy Council and, in particular, in the whipping campaign of the years 1569–72 (**2**, p. 64 **22**, pp. 80–1). In the former year there were disturbances in many parts of the country and, most serious of all, the rebellion of the Northern Earls. As the Norwich authorities were to discover, more than one local Catholic hoped to make common cause with the rebels, and they seldom lacked support from the vagrant bands. If a man was hungry and had a family to feed he could not afford to be too discriminating about his source of income; and if, as was so often the case, he had had training in arms his value would be all the greater to a potential rebel leader.

Not all men were hungry. There were some who genuinely sought trouble, as one of the articles distributed to the J.P.s of

Yorkshire shows: 'To stay the spreading of false and seditious rumours and the sending of messages from the late rebels to trouble the quiet of the realm, order is to be given in market towns and other places that all suspected passengers, vagabonds, beggars and rogues be punished with the severity and celerity, according to the late statute' (**22**, p. 81). On this occasion the Privy Council was determined that its directive should be obeyed, and there is considerable evidence that the orders were put into execution in several country districts. The justices' reports concerning vagrants for the years 1569 to 1571 are preserved from no fewer than nineteen different counties. The numbers affected obviously varied from area to area, ranging from Oxfordshire, where the justices reported that 'All things be well', to Northamptonshire, where there were apparently a number of vagrants. The general picture is one of considerable disorder, but when it is considered that many of those apprehended were either children or incapacitated in some way it seems probable that a majority of them were people in want rather than out-and-out rogues.

The purge of these years was successful in suppressing vagrancy, at least temporarily, but it did little to get at the root of the problem, which continued to be the poverty of the individual created by extraordinary circumstances. The fear of the vagrant class was still paramount when the government met to discuss the situation in 1571; fear which came to the fore with the passing of legislation more severe than in any other Act apart from the slavery statute of 1547. After first defining the vagrants as a group containing all masterless men and those not owning land, as well as certain occupations such as pedlars, tinkers and minstrels, the Act introduced into the House of Lords in 1572 ordained whipping and boring through the ear for a first offence; condemnation as a felon for a second; and the death penalty for a third. In contrast to the first Edwardian statute, there is evidence that such penalties were, in fact, enforced. In the Middlesex sessions between 1572 and 1575, for example, forty-four vagabonds were sentenced to be branded, eight to be set to service, and five to be hanged. In most cases, those hanged had previously been set to service and had run away. They were given little latitude, as the career of Joan Wynstone illustrates. She was first whipped and branded as a vagrant on 6 February 1576. The following July she was caught wandering again and only saved from hanging when her husband took her into service for two years. Still undeterred, she fled again at the first opportunity and was finally caught and sentenced to be hanged on 3 October, less than eight months from her original sentence (**2**, p. 70).

Despite the severity of these regulations, the Act of 1572 can properly be regarded as a watershed in the poor law history of the sixteenth century; for if on the one hand it reflected the oppressive outlook of the legislator who saw nothing but evil in the vagrant bands, on the other it looked forward to a system which not only recognised the presence of the able-bodied man seeking work but actually sought to provide him with some means of livelihood. The Act was very cautious about such recognition, and far more concerned to stress the classes that were actually vagrants. The net was wide, and, quite apart from the unauthorised beggar, it enmeshed such diverse individuals as the workman on strike, the poor scholar at university, the shipwrecked sailor, the fortune-teller and the proctor or collector of subscriptions. Nevertheless, there were exceptions. Provided they were properly licensed, returning soldiers and sailors were exempted from the orders. Even more significantly, so were harvest workers and servants who had been turned away or whose masters had died. No provision was made for them – whether they lived or starved depended on their own abilities – but the central government had at least recognised the fact that there were some men who were genuinely unemployed through no fault of their own. Four years later this recognition was taken a stage further with the provision of stocks of hemp, flax and iron for them to work on [**doc. 16**].

In other respects, too, the Act was more thorough than its predecessors. It finally recognised the necessity for compulsory contributions to the relief of the poor, stipulating that weekly amounts were to be exacted for their support [**doc. 15**]. Lists of the impotent and aged 'pensioners' were to be drawn up – there was no provision for the young and able – and these people were specifically forbidden to beg unless the parish was genuinely unable to support them. Any surplus funds were to be used for the provision of houses of correction for the rogues and vagabonds. The local people were expected to administer the Act, overseers of the poor being appointed annually from among the more substantial householders to assist the constables and churchwardens in their extended duties. No payment was to be given for their services, and they could not refuse such duties.

Important though the Act was, it contained nothing that had not already been tried in the larger towns. London, Ipswich and Norwich had enforced compulsory contributions to poor relief many years before this, and the Norwich scheme for the relief of its poor included all the 'innovations' that were introduced by the central government. It was perhaps not entirely coincidental that the parliamentary committee appointed to discuss the problem in 1572 included John Aldrich, the originator of the system which is discussed fully in the next section. His experience in organising the comprehensive and successful Norwich scheme would have been invaluable, and he may well have stressed the importance of providing materials for the able-bodied as well as alms for the poor, for the East Anglian city had already been successful in introducing this measure (**66**, p. 149).

The harvests and their significance

The Acts of 1572 and 1576 between them provided a workable system of poor relief that was to endure for the next twenty years. The knowledge that work was available if it was required must have turned many a poor man's thoughts away from vagrancy, and this in turn led to some diminution of the numbers roaming the countryside. Encouraged by the success of their endeavours, the governing classes turned their attention with increasing frequency to the prevention of food shortage and the high prices which invariably followed. Such intervention was extremely necessary. Corn prices could rise with alarming suddenness, mainly because of the narrowness of the area from which supplies were drawn and the often inadequate transport facilities. In such circumstances the provision of a particular area might be in the hands of very few men, and if they were unscrupulous it was quite possible for them to prevent supplies reaching the market, to buy up what was already there and to raise the price to an artificially high level. Pressure was thus brought to bear on farmers and others to make their hoarded stores available for sale; to fix maximum prices in the local markets; and promote both the purchase of corn in bulk from abroad, and to distribute it at less than cost price (**22**, p. 87).

As it happened, the Privy Council's actions coincided with more than twenty-five years of almost continually good harvests, the only bad years between 1566 and 1593 being those of 1573 and 1586. But the wisdom of their policy was never more clearly illustrated than in the latter year when food riots broke out in the west country. The government retaliated with even stricter regulations. Under Burghley's auspices, orders were sent out to all justices of the peace early in 1587 requesting them to make minute and comprehensive surveys of all corn in the possession of every citizen, and the number of persons in their household, a policy which had been adopted previously in both the 1520s and the middle years of the century, and which was to be followed again in the famine years of the 1590s (**125**; **139**, p. 106; **77**). Individual households were allowed to retain enough for their personal needs, but any surplus had to be brought to market and sold at a moderate price. The justices themselves had to be present on market days to see that the regulations were carried out. As it happened, authorities did not always need such persuasion. In Norfolk 'the poorer sort' were already 'by persuasion sarved at meaner pryces', while in Nottinghamshire the Duke of Rutland made provision for the destitute to be sold small quantities of corn at 2s. 8d. below the market price whenever a shortage threatened (**22**, p. 89).

The regulations were not confined to the provision of corn alone. Authorities were reminded of the necessity to relieve the impotent poor and to supply the able-bodied unemployed with materials to work on, and there is some evidence to show that these orders were complied with. Thus in Blithing hundred in Suffolk five hundred poor people in adjacent towns were provided with 'bred and other victuall' for a period of twenty-three weeks. In Hemlingford, in the same county, the local justices of the peace ordered the overseers to see that 'all the poore and idle persons in everie towneship and hamlet wch are able to labour and want worke be daylie set on worke . . . towards the getting of their living according also to the former orders made to that effect' (**22**, p. 90).

The harvest failure and general dearth of 1586 was unusual and it has been suggested that it was probably caused by excessive rainfall. In subsequent years the harvests were good; so good in fact that in 1592 an observer as acute as Bacon formed the opinion that England was now in a position to feed other nations. The following year, encouraged both by the bountiful harvest and the general peace of the realm, the government repealed the anti-enclosure Act of 1563 and permitted the export of wheat, provided the home price was not above 20s. a quarter (**62**, p. 38). At the same time much of the sting was taken out of the poor law Act of 1572 by the removal of the clauses relating to death, imprisonment and boring through the ear, vagrants again being subjected to the whipping punishments of 1531 (**22**, p. 73).

Ironically, the relaxation of restrictions heralded a series of appalling harvests, not only in England but throughout Europe. The continuous rains, which fell from Ireland to Silesia, led to four bad harvests in a row, that of 1596 being disastrous with the price of wheat 83 per cent above the norm. The Great Famine, to use Professor Hoskins's words, lasted for three years, and during it Tartar women are said to have eaten their own children, while the diet of German and Italian peasants ranged from cats and dogs to fungi and snakes (**62**, p. 38).

In England, the failure of the harvest drove up all other food prices, leading to riots in places as far apart as Oxfordshire and Norfolk and, even worse, to actual death from starvation in large towns such as Newcastle. Despite attempts to control prices and give relief to the areas worst affected, prices rose to phenomenal levels. In Norwich the grain prices for 1597 are set down in the city records as one of the most astonishing features of the year, wheat being sold at 7s. a bushel, rye at 6s. 4d. upwards and barley at between 2s. 9d. and 3s. (**74**, p. 221). But these prices were distinctly lower than those prevailing elsewhere. In Shrewsbury and Barnstaple, for example, they rose alarmingly to as high as 18s. and 20s. a bushel respectively (**22**, pp. 121–4). In an attempt to avert both food riots and starvation, many of the larger towns provided grain for their inhabitants, 888,660 bushels clearing the port of London alone in a period of seven months in 1596–7 (**18**, p. 93). The Shrewsbury merchants imported about 3200 bushels of corn, selling the rye at 8s. a bushel and the wheat at between 14s. and 15s. Bread was specially baked for the poor and sold at prices ranging from one penny to threepence a loaf. In Bristol one alderman alone spent £1200 on the provision of grain, and saw to it that small quantities were brought to market each day. Despite this, corn which was being sold at 6s. a bushel in 1596 rose to between 16s. and 20s., prices so obviously beyond the reach of the poor that the Bristol aldermen were ordered to provide them with one meal a day to prevent general starvation (**22**, pp. 122–4). In Norwich the prices were deliberately kept down, the 4600 quarters of imported rye being sold at 4s. a bushel, half the price prevailing in Shrewsbury. The quantity provided was more than enough for the local inhabitants, for by 1599 the authorities were complaining that unless the grain was sold quickly the city would suffer a financial loss. The burden fell mainly on the shoulders of the aldermen and councillors who were ordered to buy quantities of it, although the load was lessened to a certain extent by private citizens who wanted to replenish their own stocks (**74**, p. 223).

In country districts, many parishes found the task of maintaining the poor beyond them. Attempts were made to pass the responsibility to wealthier areas, as was done in Norwich, but the Norfolk J.P.s found it necessary to authorise licences to beg on a number of occasions (**120**; **123**). The possibility of famine led to bread riots in London and actual insurrection in both Oxfordshire and Norfolk. In the former county the rebels themselves said that they rose because of the high price of corn and the sufferings of the poor. The rising was quickly quelled, and the leader, one Bartholomew Steere, a carpenter, and about twenty others were executed, but the government feared, with reason, that spontaneous uprisings might take place in any part of the country. News of insurrection travelled incredibly quickly, and led to a ready response from others in the same circumstances. As Miss Leonard tells us: 'One of the Norfolk rioters said he had heard that the poor were up in the west country, and that four or five of his neighbours would go to a justice of the peace and desire to have corn cheap; if they could not get it reasonably they would arise and get it by force, and if they did arise they would knock down the best first' (**22**, p. 126; **18**, p. 93). Hunger was the driving force behind the disturbances in Somerset, so vividly described by Edward Hext in his letter to Burghley, and also accounts for the considerable increase in the number of vagrants in these years. All too often it coincided with, or led to, plague, and confusion piled upon confusion. All four northern counties were affected after the harvest failure of 1597, and the Bishop of Durham described to Lord Burghley how 'in the bishopric of Durham five hundred ploughs have decayed in a few years and corn has to be fetched from Newcastle, whereby the plague is spread in the northern counties. . . . Of eight thousand acres lately in tillage, now not eight score are tilled; those who sold corn have to buy . . . tenants cannot pay their rents' (**68**, pp. 82–3). It was in these circumstances, with the crisis at its height, that parliament was convened in October 1597.

The sheer weight of evidence had compelled the government to realise that there were many thousands of men, both in urban and rural areas, who were unemployed through no fault of their own; and that in future adequate provision would have to be made for these as well as for the old, the incapacitated and the unrepentantly vagrant. Not altogether surprisingly, in view of the recent dearth of corn, attacks were made again on enclosures. In Sir Francis Bacon's view they bred idleness and led to the decay of tillage, grievous poverty and a substantial impoverishment of the realm. But others were far more concerned with 'the extream and miserable estate of the godly and honest sort of the poor subjects of this realm'. Sir Francis Hastings, in particular, protested against the time and consideration being given to the old and worn subjects of enclosure and tillage at a time when vagrancy and the plight of the poor were of far greater consequence (**22**, p. 74). After considerable discussion, no fewer than seventeen separate Bills were introduced, of which eleven dealt specifically with the problem of poor relief. The titles of some of them give an idea of the many sides of the question which were discussed. Drafts were submitted for 'erecting of Houses of Correction and punishment of rogues and sturdy beggars and for levying of certain sums due to the poor'; for the 'necessary habitation and relief of the poor, aged, lame and blind in every parish'; for 'relief of Hospitals, poor prisoners and others impoverished by casual losses'; for 'the better relief of soldiers and mariners'; for 'the better governing of Hospitals and lands given to the relief of the poor'; for 'extirpation of beggary'; for 'setting the poor on work'; and for 'erecting hospitals or abiding and working houses for the poor' (**22**, p. 75). Order emerged out of chaos with the discussion of these Bills in a committee which included parliamentary leaders of the calibre of Sir Francis and Sir Nicholas Bacon, Sir Thomas Cecil, Sir Robert Wroth and Edward Hext, whose recent experiences in Somerset must have coloured the proceedings to no small degree.

While the Lower House were broadly in agreement, there was some dissension between the Commons and the House of Lords over procedure. A Bill concerning Houses of Correction was heavily amended in the Upper House and returned to the House of Commons, where it was discussed in committee. Sir Walter Raleigh, as its spokesman, proposed a conference with the Lords on the subject. This was agreed to, but was virtually nullified by the peers' insistence that their amendments could not now be altered by the Commons. After some argument, the Bill was rejected, and a new one was sent up to the Lords (**22**, p. 76).

The Acts of 1598 and 1601

Arguments notwithstanding, positive action was taken by the government over the whole issue of poverty and vagrancy. The first of a series of statutes was designed to deal with the 'professional poor', the rogues, vagabonds and sturdy beggars. Vagabondage was again carefully defined, and it was ordered that any persons thus designated were to be arrested, whipped until bloody, and then returned by the most direct route to their place of origin. If they delayed on the way they were to be whipped again. On reaching their home parish they were to be placed in service if able-bodied, or lodged in almshouses if deemed incapacitated in any way. If necessary, incorrigible rogues were to be committed to gaol or a house of correction, and the Act authorised justices of the peace to erect such places in every county and city in the kingdom. If treatment of this sort proved insufficient to deter the rogue element, provision was made for them to be banished from the realm or committed perpetually to the galleys. Any that returned from such banishment left themselves open to execution as felons (**18**, p. 95).

The evils of enclosure were again recited, and provision made for the restoration of any 'houses of husbandry' with twenty acres or more of land that had been allowed to decay or waste since the beginning of the reign. A companion Act 'for the maintenance of husbandry and tillage' ordered that all grazing lands which had been arable for a period of twelve years continuously prior to 1558 should be restored to tillage; similarly any land that had been used for grazing purposes for the past twelve years was to be maintained in that condition.

Ideally, this 'freezing' of the agricultural situation as it was at the beginning of Elizabeth's reign should have been beneficial to the poor. Protection from the evils of enclosure, assuming that such evils did in fact still exist, coupled with effective legislation can only have been beneficial to the increasing number of rural wage-earners, but in reality such a scheme was a non-starter from the outset. It was passed 'by men against whose own self-interest its prescription ran, surely with full knowledge that it was unenforceable', and in such circumstances its effect must have been minimal (**18**, pp. 95–6).

Of far greater importance, and central to the whole problem at issue, was the statute entitled 'An Act for the relief of the poor'. In itself it contained little in the way of innovation, and little that was really sweeping or bold. But it did gather together the experience of a century of trial and error, a century in which men's opinions had become progressively more humane and their minds receptive to the arguments of the politicians, whether those arguments stemmed from a cold appraisal of the facts or from a genuine desire to improve the lot of those whose sufferings were greatest. Any scheme, local or national, placed heavy reliance on the executive power, and the Act moved at once to a definition of the duties of the overseers of the poor, officials drawn from the churchwardens and 'four other substantial householders'. These people, with the consent of two or more justices of the peace, were empowered to set to work children whose parents could not provide for them, as well as everybody else with no obvious means of maintenance. All those with sufficient means were to be taxed for the provision of a supply of materials on which the poor could be set to work, and for the binding of poor children as apprentices – the boys being committed until they were twenty-four, and the girls until they were twenty-one years of age.

Despite the fact that it had been legally in operation since 1572, it was realised that taxation would involve problems, whether they stemmed from recalcitrant individuals who would have to be pushed all the way, or from people who were genuinely unable to pay. With this in mind, the statute carefully defined the functions and responsibilities of the overseers in this respect. They were required to meet monthly and at the end of each year submit a full account of their activities and finances to two justices of the peace. If they were absent without reason from such meetings, or otherwise negligent, they left themselves open to a fine of 20s. If it was apparent from their returns that any parish was unable to raise the necessary funds by taxation, then the rates were to be spread over the hundred, and in the unlikely event of this being insufficient, the justices of the peace in Quarter Sessions were authorised to rate other parishes in the county to ensure the correct working of the Act. Power was given to distrain the goods of any really recalcitrant non-payer, or, if this proved impractical, to commit him to prison until his tax was paid. The funds obtained were to be used specifically for poor relief, including the provision of suitable dwelling places for the destitute and the relief of prisoners in the King's Bench and Marshalsea. Where necessary, support was to be given to such almshouses as might need aid in each county. On the assumption that these orders would be faithfully executed, the government decreed the virtual extirpation of beggary, stipulating that 'no person shall go wandering abroad and beg in any place whatsoever, by licence or without, upon pain to be taken and punished as a rogue' (**18**, pp. 96–7).

This Act, having carefully defined responsibility for both the unemployed and unemployable poor, remained in force, in all essentials, for almost 250 years. The Statute of 1601 which followed it was, in fact, a re-enactment of that of 1597–8, with slight alterations. It made provision, for example, for the release of girls from their apprenticeships if they married before reaching the age of twenty-one; and made grandparents as well as parents the responsibility of their families. In the same year the procedure for dealing with wounded soldiers was tightened up. Provision was made for the appointment of County Treasurers who were to be responsible for the payment of pensions to all those wounded or maimed in the wars, the money for the purpose being raised by the county rate (**22** pp. 134–5).

Two further Acts, one for the erection of hospitals or workhouses for the poor and the other for defining the law of charitable trusts, completed the Elizabethan legislation in this respect. Both recognised the importance of private charity as a valuable, indeed an essential, supplement to the laws passed by the central government. In the first instance, it encouraged private benefactors who might wish to found and endow almshouses, houses of correction and similar institutions for the use of the poor, by simplifying legal procedure. In future, provided such foundations were endowed with property of the clear annual value of at least £10, donors were authorised to bequeath land or other resources by enrolling a deed in Chancery. Previously, a royal licence or Act of Parliament had been necessary to achieve such incorporation. In the case of charitable trusts, the Elizabethan statute was important not, in Professor Jordan's words, 'because it created charitable uses, but rather because it vastly stimulated constructive and well considered charitable giving by lending full and most formidable protection to the aspirations of donors'. These aspirations were wide. The preamble to the Act recalled that wealth had been left:

> . . . some for the reliefe of aged impotent and poore people, some for the maintenance of sicke and maymed souldiers and mariners, schooles of learninge, free schooles and schollers in universities, some for the repaire of bridges portes havens causewaies churches seabankes and highwaies, some for education and preferments of orphans, some for or towards reliefe stocke or maintenance for howses of correction, some for mariages of poore maides, some for supportacion ayde and helpe of younge tradesmen, handiecraftsmen and persons decayed, and others for reliefe or redemption of prisoners or captives, and for aide or ease of any poore inhabitants concerning payments of fifteens, [and] settinge out of souldiers and other taxes.

Significantly, the objectives were almost entirely secular, a single reference to repair of churches being sandwiched between 'causewaies' and 'sea-bankes'. By 1600 the total capital vested in charitable trusts in the ten counties examined by Professor Jordan had – reached £808,131 142s – a sum so vast and obviously important in the maintenance of the social order that government intervention was both wise and necessary. In an attempt to prevent the misuse of funds, the Chancellor was instructed 'to appoint commissions to enquire into abuses, to take evidence, to impanel juries and to hand down decisions subject only to his own review' (**18**, pp. 113, 119). The Act was sufficiently well thought out to remain unchanged until 1888, and even then its successor carefully preserved the preamble and its list of uses defined as charitable.

The Act of 1601 saw the completion of more than a century of experiment, ranging from the brutally repressive to the enlightened and far-sighted. All the legislation reflects the action of a government cautiously groping its way towards a method that would at once remove the threat of insurrection and provide adequate care for all categories of poor. The Tudors were not prepared to innovate in this respect. They wanted proof that methods were workable before they introduced them, and in consequence they watched the urban experiments with more than a passing interest. The larger towns, particularly London and Norwich, anticipated governmental legislation in almost every respect, and provided visible evidence of the success of more humane methods of poor relief. Their experiments are sufficiently important to be considered at length.

5 Urban Experiments in the Suppression of Vagrancy and the Relief of the Poor

London and the provincial towns

Until the end of the first decade of Elizabeth's reign, successive governments were almost entirely concerned with the suppression of the sturdy beggars. Local legislation, in contrast, went far ahead of this and, while equally concerned that the vagabonds should be kept under control, made far greater provision for the care of the indigent and the provision of work for the unemployed. Almost without exception, the laws passed by the central government in the second half of the century were based on experiments carried out by London and the larger provincial towns, particularly those in the eastern half of the country, and the success of their measures is reflected in the more humane attitude adopted at national level. While quite prepared to follow governmental legislation if it seemed adequate to deal with their particular problems, towns did not hesitate to go beyond it if necessary, and by the second decade of Elizabeth's reign many urban areas had poor law systems embodying all or much of the legislation passed in 1572, 1598 and 1601. In the majority of cases, powerful support was given to the municipal authorities by charitably disposed merchants, and, as will be seen, much of the responsibility for poor relief normally rested on their shoulders.

Not surprisingly, experimentation with poor relief began in London where the problem was at its most acute (**22**, pp. 25–40). Initially the city aldermen attempted to overcome their difficulties by providing grain for the poor at cheap rates whenever there was a bad harvest, a permanent corn stock being established in Elizabeth's reign, but following the economic dislocations of the first half of the century London had to deal with an ever-increasing influx of beggars and was obliged to go beyond what was authorised by statute to deal with them. Early in Henry VIII's reign (1514–18) able-bodied people were forbidden to beg in the city, vagrants being branded on their chest with a 'V', and an officer was appointed to keep strange beggars out of the city. The latter's task was virtually an impossible one, and by 1524 these orders were extended, sturdy beggars being whipped at the cart's tail and having collars of iron put around their necks, while the impotent poor were provided with tokens of white tin and allowed to beg within certain limits. The main provision of the statute of 1531 had thus been operating in London for some years before that date, and in 1533 the city again anticipated national legislation by arranging for house collections for poor relief, the money obtained being distributed at the church door. The dissolution of the monasteries created a temporary problem, but following appeals to the king the hospitals of St Bartholomew, St Thomas and Christ's were refounded, the first two being for the sick and impotent and the latter for children. The subsequent provision of the Bethel for the insane and the Bridewell for the sturdy beggars gave London an all-embracing system, a system that was consolidated in 1547 when it became the first town to institute compulsory payments for poor relief [**doc. 18**], sixteen years before the government took its first tentative steps in that direction and twenty-five years before the statute of 1572 clearly established such a policy. Far-sighted as the London system undoubtedly was, and despite the fact that it anticipated much of the later national legislation, it cannot be judged an unqualified success. Funds were not properly organised, there was no attempt completely to forbid begging, and the very fact that relief was given at the hospitals attracted hordes of beggars to the city instead of reducing their number.

The action taken by the capital city was extremely important, however, for it gave the central authorities an opportunity to see if such a system was working before incorporating all, or part, of it into national legislation. It also provided a basis for similar schemes in other towns. The provision of a corn stock was a common feature, Bristol and Canterbury, for example, providing one in 1522 and 1552 respectively, while Norwich had a permanent stock shortly before the beginning of Elizabeth's reign. Licensing of beggars, too, was fairly general in the first half of the century, Lincoln, Ipswich, Gloucester, Cambridge, Norwich and York all adopting this method (**22**, pp. 41–5). Generally speaking, however, provincial schemes for the relief of the poor were not undertaken until the middle of the century or even later. A number of factors may account for this: a rising population; a general increase in the level of prices; the vicissitudes of the export trade; the debasement of the coinage; even, in the short term, a successive failure of harvests such as occurred in the reign of Edward VI. Obviously not all towns were similarly affected, but it is significant that a number of them introduced poor law schemes at about the same time. The Ipswich system most nearly resembled that of London (**36**). Before 1569 the poor were surveyed and licensed there, a compulsory tax was inaugurated and a municipal hospital was erected which was all-embracing, being a House of Correction, a hospital for the old, and a training school for the young. A similar system was adopted at Cambridge, the poor first being surveyed and the impotent supported from regular contributions levied on the parish, but it was not until 1578 that attempts were made to found a hospital in the town. York, in contrast, based its poor law system in the provision of hospitals for the indigent, three being founded there under municipal management. The able-bodied poor were set to work and any income derived from the system was used for the relief of the destitute. Lincoln, too, developed a system closely resembling that of London, the citizens being forbidden to give alms to unauthorised poor as early as 1543. By 1547 the town had not only licensed its beggars but had also stipulated that they should be set to work. With adults this presented difficulties but from 1551 young people were placed with the clothiers for eight or nine years, refusal to comply resulting in banishment from the area. Finally in 1560 a special officer was appointed to deal with the poor, a post similar to that of the master of beggars appointed in London early in the sixteenth century.

If the systems of poor relief established by the various towns had been strictly adhered to, the problems of the local authorities in that respect would have been greatly diminished. Unfortunately, with the notable exception of Norwich, financial difficulties caused the collapse or virtual cessation of many of the municipal schemes, and they were further undermined by the fact that begging continued to be tolerated, even if this was theoretically confined to the impotent.

The Norwich scheme

The most successful attack on the problem of urban poverty was undoubtedly that carried out by Norwich in the decade 1570–80 (**66** *passim*). Until then the East Anglian city had had little trouble with vagabonds and was content, on the whole, to follow national legislation on the subject. When the statute of 1531 ordered that all beggars should be badged and licensed, for example, the city authorities could find no more that fifty-one of these, and there is nothing in the local records to suggest that they were unduly worried by such people. Norwich, like any other city of the time, had to deal with itinerant beggars, but these were duly whipped and given a passport to return to their place of origin, and the city's fairly rigorous settlement regulations normally prevented such people remaining in the town. It was recognised that the native poor were a prospectively dangerous element, particularly in times of distress, as was proved by their participation in Ket's Rebellion; but the authorities counteracted this danger by enforcing compulsory contributions for the relief of the poor in 1549 – apparently the first provincial town to do so – and, in common with other cities, regularly provided grain from Danzig and elsewhere when it seemed that a food shortage might prevail. In 1557 a permanent grain stock was established and a treasurer placed in charge of its funds. It is thus somewhat surprising to find the mayor, John Aldrich, complaining in 1570 that vagabonds were creating an intolerable problem in the city and inaugurating comprehensive regulations for their treatment in the future, especially as the numbers apprehended rarely exceeded twenty-five or so a year. It is quite possible that the impetus was a political one. The rebellion of the Northern Earls had taken place in the previous year and had been followed by a plot by malcontents in the Norwich area (**71**). Ostensibly, it was aimed at the increasing numbers of Dutch and Walloons settling in the neighbourhood, but the participants were chiefly Catholics and there was some talk of a link-up with the northerners it if was successful. The mayor and the local justices of the peace were aware of it from the first, and arrested the conspirators at their convenience, but the potential threat must have greatly concerned the central government. Poor men could be easily stirred up, as the events of twenty years before had proven, and it is at least possible that Aldrich was instructed to take particular care with the local destitute (**98**, pp. 8–9).

At all events, a comprehensive census was promptly taken which revealed the presence of over 2300 poor men, women and children in the city. Most claimed to follow a trade, but it was alleged that this was merely a front, the majority of them continually begging from door to door to the irritation of the citizens and the degradation of themselves. It was asserted that the local inhabitants were so beneficent in their almsgiving that many of those normally prepared to follow an occupation were taking to permanent begging as a more profitable course. They were so well supplied with food that they threw the surplus into the streets. The vagabonds among them were not concerned with permanent dwelling places but used church porches, cellars, barns and hay chambers as resting places and, as they rarely changed their clothes, most of them were disease-ridden and thus a source of physical as well as moral contagion. When not begging they spent their time in victualling places, which were filled with drunkards and abusive individuals throughout much of the day [**doc. 19**].

A number of these people may well have been permanent beggars, especially in time of extraordinary dearth, but it is far too sweeping to lump them all together in this one general category. It seems, in fact, that although speaking in general terms, the authorities were concerned with two distinct groupings of poor; the relatively passive natives and an increasing number of normally itinerant beggars drawn to the town by the generosity of its merchant class.

This viewpoint is substantiated, to some extent, by the census itself. As well as giving the occupations of all those in actual employment at the time it was taken, it specifically states which people were unemployed, differentiating between the able and those who were too old or too infirm to work. One hundred and seventy three men, or approximately one-third of the whole, were listed as being unemployed, the proportions varying from trade to trade. Forty-one of the forty-three men with no occupations to their name had no work, and some of these may represent the true beggars. Many of the building workers, too, were clearly experiencing difficulties, and rather more than half of them were unemployed at the time of the census. Elsewhere, a majority of the men in all occupations were listed as being in employment, and even where this was not the case some monetary contribution was usually made by their wives or children so that no household was entirely without income (**98**, p. 16). In addition, many of the unemployed were receiving alms at rates varying between one penny and sixpence per week. If they were all vagrants, it would have been a pointless exercise to distinguish so carefully between the employed and the unemployed, and it must be assumed that some two-thirds of the men and almost all of the women were in at least temporary employment at the time of the census.

This is not to suggest that any of this section of the community were comfortably off. Some of them may well have resorted to begging on occasion, a few may have found it more profitable to beg than work, but the very fact that the more unruly elements were stated to be homeless makes it clear that they were professional vagrants. All of the poor referred to in the census had shelter of some kind. Three hundred of them were housed in civic or church property but the remainder, totalling rather more than 2000, were in private property, whether their own or other people's. Sixty-one of the poor were owner-occupiers, one man owning two houses, another three; between them they housed a further 289 people. Significantly, almost 60 per cent of the houses containing the city's poor belonged to freemen of the city, some 36 per cent of them being aldermen and common councillors. Many of these people were multiple owners and the fact that they were prepared to rent their houses in this way suggests either blatant hypocrisy and a total disregard for the city's ordinances concerning settlement of poor newcomers; or, as suggested above, the simple fact that there was a clear-cut division between the native poor, who were in many cases able to contribute to their own welfare, and the itinerant vagrant (**98**, pp. 13–15).

Whether political events forced the city's hand or not, it seems fairly clear that the action of the Norwich authorities was taken as much with a view to the future as to deal with an immediate problem. It almost certainly reflects their anxiety at the results of the misplaced generosity of certain of the merchant class, a generosity which made it increasingly difficult to prevent beggars settling in the city, and which might ultimately corrupt the native poor and undermine what had been until then a relatively satisfactory poor law system. The action taken was drastic. It incorporated all aspects prevailing in other towns, but in four major respects it went much further. Begging of any kind was absolutely forbidden within the city precincts; an all-embracing organisation was provided which dealt adequately with every aspect of poor relief, including the provision of work for the able-bodied; regular funds were provided which were essential for the smooth running of the system; and finally, and perhaps most important of all, the city's system was consistently applied throughout the decade 1570–80, and at least intermittently thereafter. These aspects combined to give Norwich a poor law system far in advance of its contemporaries, for it was here that other towns failed most noticeably. Financial difficulties caused the collapse or virtual cessation of many of the municipal schemes, and the fact that begging was tolerated, even if theoretically confined to the impotent, undermined much of their efforts.

The financial aspect was of primary importance. A beginning

was made by trebling the existing sums donated for poor relief and, where necessary, by taxing people for the first time. Everybody who was capable of contributing was expected to do so, and the city's net was sufficiently wide to enmesh twenty of those actually recorded in the census itself, thirteen of whom, surprisingly enough, were already contributors (**77**). The assessments varied from one halfpenny to 1s. 4d. a week. As might be expected, most people paid small amounts, almost two-thirds contributing twopence or less. In contrast, all of the city aldermen had to pay one shilling a week and the Bishop of Norwich was one of the few assessed at the maximum amount.

The wealthiest parishes naturally had the largest numbers of contributors and the smallest number of poor to deal with, for there was a tendency for the less wealthy to congregate in certain areas of the city. Thus a parish such as St Peter Mancroft, with 111 people contributing to the poor rate and with only twenty-two individuals considered worthy of support, was expected to provide for the poor of other parishes as well as its own, and did in fact make contributions to six other areas. St Andrew's, with fifty-four contributors and only six of its own poor to look after, made donations to four other parishes. Altogether nine of the Norwich parishes supported their less fortunate fellows.

Within a few years of its inception, the numbers of contributors and recipients had become roughly stabilised. Throughout most of the 1570s some 950 people were providing support for about 380 regular 'pensioners'. By 1574–5 the annual receipts for poor relief exceeded £530 and they continued to be above £500 for the rest of the decade. The Norwich chamberlains (financial officials) received less than this for normal city business, a fair indication of how seriously the problem of the poor was regarded. In normal circumstances the numbers contributing were sufficiently high for the deacons to collect more than they actually paid out, and this surplus was used as a reserve stock to be drawn on in cases of special need. The usual beneficiaries were people who were sick, or who were suffering from broken limbs. Such people would not be permanent pensioners, and their ability to draw what amounted to unemployment or sickness benefit removed any excuse they may have had to beg.

The financial aspect was an absolute prerequisite if the city's system of poor relief was to be a success. Once this was established to their satisfaction, the authorities made a thorough reorganisation of the existing system. Vagabonds were placed in the Bridewell, which had been purchased for the purpose in 1565. Certain of the begging women and some of the younger children were put in the charge of 'select women' who were specially appointed for the task. Other young people were sent to St Giles's Hospital to be educated. The aged and impotent were sustained by increasing alms and, where possible, work was provided for those able and willing to do it.

A number of new officials were appointed at the same time to see that the scheme worked smoothly. The mayor himself took over the position of Master of the Bridewell and four of the aldermen were made responsible for the four great wards, or major administrative areas, of the city. They, in turn, appointed a host of minor officials. From the point of view of overall responsibility, the deacons were by far the most important of these. Two were appointed for each petty ward (twenty-four in all) and they were initially responsible for recording the names of all the poor, including those of children whose parents were unable to support them adequately, the latter being put out to service. Those with less than three years, residence were sent away from the city while all newcomers unable to support themselves were refused admittance. Having obtained this information, the deacons were ordered to see that all capable of work did work, any vagabonds, idlers, loiterers or drunkards that remained being punished. In addition to these punitive duties, they were expected to know how many poor there were in the city with insufficient alms, so that they could be provided for, and to see that any money, wood or other gifts to the poor were duly distributed.

The Bridewell, which was an essential part of the city's poor law system, was also provided with new officials. The most important was a resident bailiff who was appointed at a salary of £30 a year. From this he was expected to provide for his wife, children, servants and a surveyor who was responsible for the arrest of idle rogues. He was assisted by two wardens who were concerned with the provision of household utensils and the year's supply of food. Twelve vagabonds were to be housed in the Bridewell for a period of at least twenty-one days and obliged to work from 5 a.m. to 8 p.m. in the summer and from 7 a.m. to 6 p.m. in the winter. Half an hour was to be allowed for a meal break and quarter of an hour for prayer, and it was expressly ordered that if they refused to work they were to receive no food.

The 'select women' were appointed at a salary of 20*s* a year. Each woman was to be responsible for between six and twelve people, and while primarily responsible for seeing that they worked she was also expected to teach the children the rudiments of reading and writing. If this task was done properly, and if the evidence of the census of the poor is to be believed, it would suggest that something like one in ten of the poorer children received at least a basic education, and that the level of literacy among these people was higher than is generally believed. The women and children worked shorter hours than the men. In the winter months they began at 8 a.m. and continued until 4 p.m., while in the summer months their hours of labour extended from 6 a.m. until 'paste vii of the clocke at nighte'. Throughout the year they had a two-hour dinner break which extended from 11 a.m. to 1 p.m. Provided they supplied their own materials the women and children were allowed to keep the profits made from them. Otherwise, they had to be content with the wages paid them by the 'select women'. Although their treatment seems to have been relatively mild for the times, some unruliness was expected, for the 'select women' were empowered to give loiterers six stripes with a whip, and if they retaliated the deacons were to be called in to administer a double punishment or to send the offenders to the Bridewell.

These orders made provision for the most unruly inhabitants of Norwich, but the stipulations were by no means entirely coercive. The authorities went out of their way to provide instruction in reading and writing for the children sent to St Giles's Hospital, for example. Twelve children were to be kept there in the charge of the bailiff and his wife, who were responsible for teaching them letters and other exercises 'as their capacities shall be hable to attayne'. They were also to provide them with clothes, meat and drink and see that they went to church on Sundays. Provision was also made for the impotent poor and those prepared to work, two hospitals being maintained for the former and stocks of material being provided for the latter.

The Norwich authorities were not content to rest on their laurels. They not only maintained the existing scheme, but added to it at intervals throughout the decade 1570–80. Some of the action taken was specifically geared to avoid a return to wholesale vagrancy. A law passed in 1574, for example, stipulated that all unemployed men were to assemble at the Market Cross at 5 a.m. each day with the tools of their trade and wait there for an hour in the hope of being employed. Further laws were passed to prevent the housing of vagrants, and the city authorities dealt promptly with complaints that artisans were losing money by appearing on juries by ordering that in future they should be paid at the rate of twopence per man. Rigorous settlement regulations were enforced, any newcomers that appeared at all likely to be a charge to the city being refused admittance At the other extreme, all affluent newcomers were brought before the mayor after 1576 to be assessed for their contribution to the relief of the poor. The reserve fund was regularly drawn on to sustain people who were temporarily incapacitated, and on occasion the city went beyond this, supplementing the alms given for poor relief by making grants in kind. Thus in 1580 a lame boy was supplied with a joint of mutton or veal twice a week, as well as being treated by a surgeon. The 'medical staff' itself was improved in 1573 by the appointment of one Richard Durrant – 'a man very skillful in bone setting and of good will to dwell in the cittie' – as the municipal bonesetter. He was to be responsible 'for the releyfe of souch as shall fortune by misfortune to have ther legges, armes, or the bones of other partes of ther lymes to be broken and of souche as be poore and not able to pay for ther heling'. Durrant was obviously an able man. His initial salary of £4 a year was soon increased to £10 and he seems to have built up a clientele of private patients as well. At his death in 1602 he left bequests amounting to £282. 10s.

It would be misleading to suggest that the Norwich scheme, excellent though it was, was infallible. From time to time itinerant beggars proved themselves a nuisance, but references to them in the Court Books are far fewer than in the period before 1570 and the authorities were clearly well in command of the situation. After the scheme had been operating for a year the officials concerned reported on its success. They were able to state that throughout the year 950 children had earned 6d. a week, 64 men 1s. a week, and 180 women between 1s. and 2s. 6d. a week, all of whom, it was alleged, had previously been beggars. It was calculated that if the yearly earnings of these people were added to the sums previously given in alms, both for healing and general maintenance, the city had benefited by more than £3000. Much of this transformation was attributed to the 'feare of the terrour of the house of Bridewell', the vagrants apparently preferring to seek normal employment rather than be compelled to work in such a place. The figures for the children are almost certainly exaggerated, representing as they do virtually the total number recorded in the census, but those given for the men and women are probably correct and may well represent the numbers of known beggars among the poorer classes. Even allowing for possible over-exuberance where the figures are concerned, the scheme was clearly a success. The Norwich authorities had succeeded in just those respects that had caused, and were to cause, the collapse of so many apparently sound urban schemes. They had forbidden begging entirely, thus preventing any abuse of the licensing system; before parliamentary sanction had been given for compulsory taxation for poor relief, Norwich had not only taxed its citizens in this respect but had trebled the initial contributions and regularly collected and distributed such sums of money throughout the whole of the decade 1570–80; and provision was made for all categories of poor, even to the extent of finding work for the able-bodied. Perhaps the most significant thing about the Norwich scheme, however, was the consistency with which it was applied, and it was this consistency, above all else, which made it superior to those undertaken by other towns, and ultimately brought the city national acclaim. Matthew Parker, the Archbishop of Canterbury, and himself a Norwich man, specifically asked for details of the Norwich methods, and John Aldrich, its originator, sat on a parliamentary committee which discussed the whole issue of poor relief in 1572. It is perhaps more than a coincidence that the Act passed in that year incorporated several aspects of the Norwich scheme.

During 1579 and 1580 Norwich was decimated by plague, and the official records of its poor law administration cease in the latter year. The poor law officials continued to be appointed, however; the Bridewell remained operative; and the surviving accounts for fourteen of the city's parishes show that a poor rate was being levied throughout the seventeenth century and beyond. It is at least possible that the compulsory rates first introduced in 1549, and still clearly in operation in 1570 before the city revised its poor law policy, were levied regularly thereafter; and that Norwich may represent one of the few examples – possibly the only example – where a poor rate was in continuous operation from the mid sixteenth century onwards.

The Norwich scheme for the relief of its poor merits attention for a number of reasons. Its longevity has already been pointed out. The city records are especially full, and the picture which emerges from them is far more comprehensive than could be painted from similar sources elsewhere. This is particularly true where the details of the poor themselves are concerned. Finally, and perhaps most important of all, it was a scheme which involved wholesale participation, literally everybody who was capable of contributing being called upon to do so. The charities set up by the Norwich merchants were a valuable supplement to the system, and ensured that many less affluent tradesmen kept their heads above water, but the city never relied entirely on such assistance. In contrast, Professor Jordan has pointed out that in normal circumstances many towns were wholly reliant on their merchant classes, and only resorted to the provisions of the various statutes in times of extreme emergency.

6 The Contribution of the Individual

The various urban schemes, followed, after a short interval, by governmental legislation, provided the machinery for at least an adequate system of poor relief by the end of Elizabeth's reign. Insufficient funds, combined with municipal apathy, however, meant that such schemes were rarely invoked except in cases of extreme emergency. It has been pointed out that taxation provided no more than 7 per cent of the vast sums spent on poor relief before 1660, and, although contributions were theoretically compulsory after 1572, the city fathers continued to find it difficult to enforce the law (**18**, p. 140). Immediately prior to the passing of the great Elizabethan poor law in 1601, a city as enlightened as Norwich still had to resort to persuasion in an attempt to keep its vagrancy problem within reasonable bounds (**66**, p. 151). The East Anglian city was successful, but smaller towns without the same traditions or organisation could not hope to match it in this respect and their pleas invariably fell on stony ground.

Merchant philanthropy

In normal circumstances, much of the responsibility for the maintenance of the local poor devolved on the mercantile community, a fact which is brought out clearly from a study of their wills. As a class, they had always been lavish in their bequests, being particularly generous in the period 1480 to 1540. The actual scale of giving never again approached the pre-Reformation level but, what was far more important, the direction of giving changed radically. Before the Reformation 45 per cent of London charity was devoted to religious purposes: by the end of the century the Church was receiving as little as 7 per cent, and what happened in London was reflected to a greater or lesser extent elsewhere. The chief gainers were the destitute. Inspired partly by the working of an uneasy conscience, partly by the fear of social disorder, the merchants became acutely aware of the problem of poverty and they made a ready response to oratory from the pulpit. In the second half of the sixteenth century they fulfilled their obligations to society in this respect both by subscribing to the poor rate and by bequeathing sums of money from a few shillings to several pounds. Even more important, in many cases they left directions for the establishment of charitable trusts. It was in this latter respect that the mercantile contribution was really decisive, since it made provision not only for immediate needs but for future contingencies as well.

If only by virtue of their numerical superiority, the sums provided by the merchants for the relief of the poor far outweighed those of any other class in society. For practically the whole of the sixteenth century, they provided succour for six people out of every ten, only falling below this level in the Elizabethan period when they turned their attention increasingly to the problem of social rehabilitation. Even then they contributed 56 per cent of the available funds. In the sixty years between 1480 and 1540 they bequeathed some £29,737 towards the relief of the poor. Between 1541 and 1560 they made available a further £23,796 and this sum was virtually trebled during Elizabeth's reign when no less than £68,479 was donated for this purpose (Table 1). This is not to say that they were sustaining three times as many people. In a period of steadily rising prices, due account must always be taken of inflation, but their contribution remains impressive, particularly as they were concerned with far more than immediate poor relief. Funds set up in many of the major cities made provision not only for the destitute but also for needy artisans who were in temporary financial difficulties. Nevertheless, there was no sentimentality about such provision. Where the poor were concerned, it was intended to keep a family from starvation and very little else, and it was anticipated that the recipients would find full or, at the very least, supplementary employment at the earliest opportunity. The trusts were also unevenly distributed. In Somerset, for example, 84 per cent of the charitable funds were concentrated in 9 per cent of the parishes (**75**, p. 327). This was extreme, but in the country as a whole something like one-third of the parishes in each area were worse off than their neighbours. It was here that real suffering was most likely to occur and where private charity was at its least successful. Large towns, such as Exeter, Ipswich and Norwich, combated the problem by arranging for the wealthier parishes to subsidise the poorer. In times of real distress, many of the authorities had no alternative but to implement the statutes, but this was regarded as an essentially emergency measure and they reverted to parochial assistance as soon as it was practicable to do so. Where the poorer tradesmen were concerned, the objective was prevention rather than cure. Funds were made available for those who lacked the capital to set up in business, or who were in other financial difficulties, and might easily become progressively poorer. The really destitute were in no position to take advantage of such opportunities, for at least a little security was demanded, and the merchants invariably had in mind the needier members of their own particular occupations. The very existence of such funds, however, ensured that the problem of poverty never got out of hand, and that the really needy were always maintained at a manageable level.

The merchants were never concerned with the maintenance of the poor alone. Throughout the century many of them, particularly those from Bristol and London, were almost equally interested in the allied problem of social rehabilitation. Their interests in this respect were wide. The provision of loan funds has already been mentioned. They were also concerned with the welfare of prisoners, especially those imprisoned for debt; the endowment of apprenticeships, an aspect which assumed particular importance towards the end of Elizabeth's reign; the provision of stocks of materials for the poor in the workhouses; the care of the sick, especially where the foundation or refoundation of hospitals was concerned; and, to a much lesser degree, with the provision of marriage portions for poor girls (**18**, pp. 263 *et seq.*). The merchants were virtual pioneers in the field of social rehabilitation. In the pre-Reformation period they provided almost 93 per cent of the funds that were donated for this purpose, their £8830 being thirteen times as great as the combined contributions of the other classes. In the middle years of the century they provided three-quarters of the funds, and during Elizabeth's reign their share rose to just under 87 per cent (Table 1). In the process they made available six times as much capital as they had done during the years 1541 to 1560, a significant increase even when full allowance has been made for inflation. They had no serious rivals in this field, the only time they were remotely challenged being in the middle decades of the century. By any standards, their contribution was impressive and a worthwhile and important supplement to their interest in poor relief.

Table 1. The contributions of the various classes to the relief of the poor and to social rehabilitation

	Total bequeathed									Percentage of all bequests		
	1480–1540			1541–1560			1561–1600			1480–1540	1541–1560	1561–1600
	£	s	d	£	s	d	£	s	d			
To relief of the poor												
Nobles	3,578	16	0	813	6	0	8,989	1	0	7.21	2.60	7.95
Upper gentry	4,180	16	0	3,464	13	0	8,485	14	0	8.41	8.78	7.54
Lower gentry	5,137	5	0	2,047	18	0	15,397	8	0	10.12	5.20	12.64
Yeomen	756	8	0	1,045	12	0	6,693	13	0	1.53	2.65	5.50
Husbandmen	27	11	0	178	7	0	407	12	0	–	0.45	0.33
Lower clergy	1,282	11	0	1,908	4	0	1,341	13	0	2.60	4.84	1.10
Merchants	29,737	0	0	23,796	6	0	68,479	5	0	60.27	60.34	56.04
Tradesmen	4,145	17	0	5,926	4	0	11,231	13	0	8.40	15.21	9.22
Artisans	481	5	0	255	16	0	780	10	0	0.98	0.65	0.64
TOTALS	49,327	9	0	39,436	6	0	121,806	9	0	Approximately 100%		
To social rehabilitation												
Nobles	45	0	0	45	0	0	1,130	0	0	0.47	0.39	1.86
Upper gentry	123	11	0	130	17	0	1,444	18	0	1.39	1.15	2.38
Lower gentry	161	7	0	109	1	0	1,394	13	0	1.70	0.96	2.31
Yeomen	30	12	0	59	9	0	154	17	0	0.33	0.52	0.26
Husbandmen	10	15	0		1	0		17	0	0.11	–	–
Lower clergy	114	9	0	150	6	0	323	1	0	1.20	1.32	0.53
Merchants	8,830	5	0	8,782	7	0	52,498	1	0	92.85	77.33	86.71
Tradesmen	132	14	0	2,052	19	0	3,496	14	0	1.39	18.71	5.77
Artisans	61	7	0	27	3	0	172	12	0	0.66	0.24	0.28
TOTALS	9,509	10	0	11,357	3	0	60,615	12	0	Approximately 100%		

Figures from Jordan (**18**, pp. 385–7); totals and percentages calculated by the present writer

Other classes

The importance of the merchant class – numerically the largest, it must be remembered – in the fields of both poor relief and social rehabilitation is undeniable. Nevertheless, it would be a rank injustice to ignore the efforts of other members of the social strata, and it would not be disparaging the efforts of the merchants if rather greater stress was laid on the equally deserving contribution of the other classes. Without exception, there was a general swing away from donating to the Church and a far greater tendency to leave money for the relief of the poor. In most cases the changeover was rapid. In others it was more gradual, but even the most conservative of the groups – the husbandmen – were leaving almost 70 per cent of their charitable bequests to poor relief by the end of the century, whereas at the beginning the bulk of their donations went for religious purposes. It is perhaps worth stressing that during the entire period under consideration between four and five people out of every ten were supported by classes other than the merchants.

Even allowing for the undoubted effects of inflation, the increasing interest of the tradesmen in the care of the poor in general and in social rehabilitation in particular during the Reformation period is significant. Influenced in all probability by the wealthier merchants, their bequests, on paper at least, show a fifteenfold increase in the latter respect while those of the merchants remain virtually static. In the Elizabethan era, when contributions to poor relief in general showed a marked increase, the tradesmen supplied almost 10 per cent of the funds for this purpose, and they were the only class, apart from the merchants, to make a sizeable contribution to social rehabilitation, their £3500 providing support for just over one person in every twenty.

The nobility and gentry, taken together, also made an extremely important contribution to poor relief, their bequests accounting for something like one-quarter of the available funds. Their interest in social rehabilitation, too, showed a marked increase in Elizabeth's reign. In the middle decades of the century, their total bequests for this purpose amounted to only £285, but in the following forty years they increased this to just under £3970, or about 6 per cent of the whole (Table 1). But this interest is reflected entirely in their bequests and does scant justice to the role played by both the nobility and the gentry in their lifetime. As Professor Wilson has pointed out, 'the possession of land, manorial rights and an assured traditional place in the social hierarchy conferred opportunities for informal and unrecognised charity by the lord and his lady which were not open to the merchant' (**76**, p. 687). People of this class were expected to live a life of ceaseless charity, giving in both money and kind. In 1489 over 13,000 poor people received a twopenny dole at the funeral of the fourth Earl of Northumberland. A century later between three and four thousand poor were fed from the left-overs from the feast of Edward, Earl of Rutland, and over a thousand were similarly treated at the feast of Lady Berkeley in 1596. These are simply isolated examples taken from Professor Stone's monumental work on the aristocracy and the number of unrecorded cases must be legion (**31**, p. 575).

If the nobility and gentry must not be ignored, neither must the yeomen. As a class they were preoccupied with the needs of the poor, almost 60 per cent of their bequests being intended for this purpose. Their contribution was far from negligible. In Elizabeth's reign they provided almost 6 per cent of the available capital, but the £6693 they donated would have provided relief for more than the one person in twenty that this suggests (Table 1). They were essentially concerned with the poor of their own immediate locality, and where, as was so often the case, there was no local squire, their interest was paramount. Willingly or unwillingly, they contributed to the poor rate in their lifetime – a charge which was not necessarily infrequent, as F. G. Emmison has shown in his studies of Essex and Bedfordshire – and their work as parish constables and overseers of the poor made them particularly aware of the problem of poverty in their own areas (**53, 54**). In consequence, they tended to seek immediate solutions. In virtually every case they made provision for direct household relief and they had little interest in social rehabilitation. In the case of the wealthier yeomen, their interest may well have extended beyond the payment of rates and the provision of charity after their deaths. At this level they merged imperceptibly with the lesser gentry, and there is no reason to assume that they did not accept at least some of the same responsibilities. By virtue of their status they would have been able to avoid unnecessary ostentation, but this would not have precluded their making extraordinary contributions to poor relief as and when they considered it fit to do so.

Moving to a lower level, it would not be unfair to say that the contributions of the husbandmen and artisans were a mere drop in the ocean compared to the vast sums left by their wealthier contemporaries. But even these tiny sums must not be entirely ignored, for almost 70 per cent of their bequests was intended for the relief of the local poor, and in communities as small as this, the least of the 'widows' mites' would have had an important role to play.

All the classes dealt with so far, from the wealthiest merchant to the humblest artisan, displayed an intense interest in the relief to the poor. It is thus more than a little surprising to find the clergy, the one class that one would have expected to be particularly concerned, displaying what amounts to palpable indifference to one of the central problems of the age. The upper clergy – the bishops and abbots – were so little concerned that they bequeathed no more than 10 per cent of their funds for this purpose, the bulk of it being devoted to the foundation of almshouses. The amount allotted to household relief was smaller still, comprising less than 4 per cent of their total bequests. The lower clergy were more generous, but only in a relative sense, just over one-quarter of their bequests being devoted to poor relief. The numbers supported by these bequests, with the possible exception of the period 1541–60, were minimal. During the reign of Elizabeth, when more and more people were turning their attention to the problem of the poor, the donations of the lower clergy amounted to little more than 1 per cent of the available capital (Table 1). This is particularly difficult to understand for, as Professor Jordan says, 'they worked and lived closely with the poor, exhorted their congregations to acts of charity, and could not have escaped from the harsh realities of the problem with which all classes of the realm were engaged' (**18**, p. 348).

If one takes the contribution of the various classes as a whole, then the role of private charity as an agent of poor relief was clearly one of considerable importance. It now seems absolutely clear, however, that it was not as important as Professor Jordan originally suggested. His claim that little more than £12,000 was obtained from the local rates for the relief of the poor is clearly an underestimate. In the decade 1570–80 alone, Norwich was spending in excess of £500 a year on poor relief, all derived from local rates, and both before and after that period a well-organised rating system was in existence (**66**). In the same period. the neighbouring town of Ipswich was obtaining between £170 and £195 a year from the local poor rate, and the surviving records suggest that this may have been in operation for some years (**36**, pp. 46, 147). The poor rate provided the main source of income for the relief of the poor in practically every parish in rural Shropshire, although in the town of Ludlow itself private charity was apparently of greater signifi-

cance (**144**, pp. 211 and 272). There seems no reason to suggest
that these areas were unique in this respect, and it seems highly
likely that the amounts derived from the poor rate in the country
as a whole were far larger than Professor Jordan assumed, particularly as more and more material is coming to light from the parish
chests [**doc. 20**]. The researches of Messrs Bittle, Lane and
Hadwin have made it equally clear that the arguments advanced
in favour of private charity must be considerably modified,
especially when this is considered as a proportion of national
income. The first two writers have gone so far as to suggest that,
in real terms, it was negligible (**117** and **118**). Mr Hadwin, in
contrast, has argued that if full account is taken of inflation, the
yield of private benefactors had doubled by the middle years of the
sixteenth century and had increased by a further 50 per cent by its
end. This was sufficient to keep it ahead of the rising population,
but in terms of the current national income he has suggested that
what is most noticeable in Jordan's 'explosion of giving' is the
whimper rather than the bang (**127**, pp. 112 and 117).

Nevertheless, when all is said and done, it is undeniable that the
role of private charity in relieving the poor, and not only in
relieving them but in preventing others from sliding into the same
abyss, was of some significance in Tudor England. Without at least
the relative generosity of the merchant class and, to a lesser extent,
other groups in society, Tudor governments would have found the
problem of poor relief far more onerous than in fact it was, and the
burden might well have become insupportable.

Part Three: Assessment

Any attempt to put the problem of poverty and vagrancy into perspective must begin with a reminder of the dimensions of that problem. It is undeniable that the numbers of poor, as such, were large. Between them, they comprised anything from 50 to 60 per cent of the population of any area of reasonable size, and on occasion their numbers were higher still. They ranged from the absolutely destitute to the wage-earner. Between one-quarter and one-third of the population were considered to be too poverty-stricken to be assessed for taxation purposes in the period 1523 to 1527, and of those that were taxed, up to 40 per cent were assessed on wages of 20s. a year. The wage-earner's position was a tenous one. Any one of a host of factors could reduce his purchasing power, and a man who was maintaining himself at one moment might find himself without visible means of support at the next [doc. 6].

The rural labourer was better off than his urban counterpart in this respect, for whereas a town-dweller seldom had any alternative means of support, a countryman could often supplement his earnings from the produce of such land as he possessed. This was seldom large. Two out of three labourers had little more than a garden, with possibly a small close attached, and as the century progressed their share of the cultivable area of the country as a whole was declining. Holdings varied from area to area. In Sussex and some of the more densely populated parts of East Anglia between 75 and 80 per cent of the peasant proprietors had less than one acre of land. Just over 60 per cent were in a similar position in Yorkshire and Lancashire and 57 per cent in the eastern part of Northamptonshire. In 1608 at Hartest in Suffolk, there were no fewer than 'forty small and poor copyholders, the best of them not having above two acres, the most of them being cottingers, and 35 other poor households that have no habitation of their own, nor cow nor calf' (55, p. 405). In such circumstances, they had little alternative but to turn to by-employments, such as spinning and weaving, to maintain themselves at a reasonable level, particularly as the cost of living rose twice as quickly as wages. During the period 1500 to 1640, despite a threefold increase in monetary terms, real wages dropped by as much as 50 per cent. Those who had to rely on wages alone, and their number increased as the century progressed, invariably found themselves in real difficulties, and their plight was made worse by the fact that there was no guarantee of regular employment. Such circumstances bred animosity between employer and employee, and the occasional threats that were uttered against the propertied classes did little to reassure an already nervous government.

Nevertheless, it was an unfortunate farm labourer who was unable to avail himself of common rights, which in moorland and woodland districts were often extensive. Labourers could make use of shrubs, woods, undergrowth, stone quarries and gravel pits; in parts of Lancashire they were allowed to dig what coal they pleased, and in the eastern parts of Kent labourers were allowed loam and sand to make bricks for their houses. In the Isle of Axholme they had the rights of fishing and fowling; in Hatfield Chase they could almost live off the rabbits on the common; while in other areas hares, fish, wood-pigeons and birds' eggs made up the working man's diet. 'Almost every living thing in the parish, however insignificant, could be turned to some good use by the frugal peasant farmer or his wife' (**55**). It was a very poor labourer, too, who possessed no stock whatsoever. According to the evidence of inventories taken at their deaths, as few as one in twenty was in that position before 1600. Most of them possessed cattle, the proportion ranging from 55 per cent in the west country to as high as 75 per cent in the east. Something like half of the peasants in the Midlands and East Anglia kept swine; sheep were reared by 20 per cent of the East Anglian labourers and by up to half of those living in the Midlands. Smaller numbers kept horses, hens and geese. The majority of farm labourers had no more than two beasts and the number of those with more than five animals never rose above 6 per cent, but the combination of common rights and a few animals meant that absolute poverty could usually be avoided except in the most exceptional circumstances.

The really destitute in a rural parish were usually supported without any difficulty, a fact which becomes abundantly clear as more and more churchwardens' and overseers' accounts are unearthed from the parish chests. When necessary, the requisite sums of money were collected regularly. If few, or none, were deemed worthy of support, then the collections were allowed to lapse or the money was used for other purposes. From time to time, every parish benefited from windfalls in the form of bequests from local benefactors or even from those living further afield, and most of the local poor had occasional donations from the local gentry and the wealthier yeomen. Sometimes extraordinary forms of taxation were devised. Thus in 1599 at Bunwell in Norfolk 106 people were assessed at the rate of one penny for each acre of land owned, with the intention of providing stocks of materials for the local poor, and fifty of them paid a further penny for each six acres owned to provide support for the impotent. In consequence, two seventy-year-olds and twenty-two children under twelve were maintained from the rates and thirty able-bodied unemployed were provided with materials to work on (**77**). North Walsham, in the same county, had ten regular pensioners between 1563 and 1588, rather more than 100 of the inhabitants being rated for their support at irregular intervals (**77**). Similar numbers were maintained at various places in both Essex and Bedfordshire and, almost certainly, throughout the rest of the country. It was only in the famine years of the 1590s that these measures proved inadequate.

Urban poverty was another thing entirely, and posed far greater problems for the authorities concerned. Quite apart from the fact that few wage-earners had alternative sources of income, professional vagrants as well as some of the rural unemployed were drawn to the towns in the hope of either easy pickings or possible employment. Some, at least, did very well for themselves if the examples of Nicholas Gennings and Mother Arden are at all typical, and any beggar who could afford to throw food into the streets, as was alleged by the Norwich authorities, was very far removed from starvation [**doc. 19**]. Obviously, not all were as lucky as this. Textile workers, in particular, were the victims of intermittent industrial depression. Periods of unemployment could be lengthy and if these coincided with harvest failure or the onset of plague the results could be disastrous. Three-quarters of the sixteenth century had passed before any real provision was made for the able-bodied unemployed, and the government's determination to persecute all but the aged and impotent must, on occasion, have caused very real distress.

The action of the central government was dictated by fear. Every Tudor monarch had to contend with at least one serious rising and, not insignificantly, every decade from the 1530s onwards saw at least one Act directed towards the relief of the poor and the suppression of vagrancy. Suppression is the key word. Any master-less man was deemed potentially dangerous and the greater the national emergency the more severe were the laws passed against the unemployed. It is not entirely a coincidence that the minority of Edward VI saw the introduction of the most savage vagrancy laws of the century. It took a further three decades before the central authorities realised that the problem needed to be tackled at its roots and that the provision of work was a far greater panacea for ills than the threat of whipping and ultimate death. The towns moved more quickly than the government in this respect and in some, such as London, Ipswich and Norwich, very full provision had been made for all classes of impotent poor by the middle years of the century. In London and Norwich this provision included compulsory assessments for poor relief. Even so, it was not until the East Anglian city reorganised its system of poor relief in 1570 that any real provision was made for the unemployed artisans.

Until such provision was made, an unemployed man with no reserves to call on had two choices, to beg or to starve. If he genuinely desired work rather than charity, and if the prospects appeared to be limited in his own locality, he might prefer to seek employment elsewhere. Several men in this position would soon swell the bands of local vagrants, and many of those with good intentions at the outset found themselves permanently following such a life. Apart from the out-and-out criminal element among them – those that used violence and, on occasion, resorted to murder – these people were little more than a nuisance. A proportion of them were whipped according to statute, a proportion which rose or fell depending on the activity of the Privy Council or the state of the economy, but they seldom stretched the local con-stabulary. Their numbers were largely governed by the success or failure of industrial activity in given areas or, to a lesser extent, by the known generosity of individual towns. If the monasteries were particularly lavish in the distribution of alms, hosts of beggars would be drawn to the locality, as the Duke of Norfolk found in Yorkshire when 'mopping up' after the Pilgrimage of Grace [**doc. 4**], but it would be wrong to assume that this was a nation-wide phenomenon. Similarly, reports of increasing numbers of beggars in areas temporarily affected by industrial depression should not be interpreted as a permanent increase in the numbers of these people. Even the great and very real distress caused by the disastrous harvests of the late 1590s was a temporary phenomenon, although in this case it finally brought home to the government the absolute necessity of providing alternative sources of employment as well as ensuring adequate supplies of grain.

Nevertheless the men on the spot reported the situation as they saw it. To the Duke of Norfolk in the north of England in the 1530s who 'never saw so many [beggars] as in these countries' [**doc. 4**]; to a man like Hext, sixty years later, faced with the visible evidence of a great increase in the number of vagrants, with the knowledge that they were becoming bolder, that some were armed, and that they could occasionally sway the course of justice [**doc. 7**]; to local authorities who had to hang them in droves whenever their numbers increased, vagrancy was a problem of major proportions. To the central government who had to combat a rising, often of some seriousness, every ten years, the beggars were dangerous as prospective adherents of the rebels. But with the exception of periods of acute famine, vagrancy was seldom a serious national problem. There were, of course, beggars throughout the country, whether they were out of work artisans or professional rogues, but this is not to say that they caused the local authorities any major difficulties. When difficulties did occur, it was almost always at local level and mainly as the result of industrial depression. The Suffolk rising of 1525 is a classic example of this, but it was suppressed with relative ease even though it did involve action at high level. Local farmers and justices of the peace were irritated, even at times molested, by wandering rogues, especially when soldiers and sailors were demobilised, but never to the extent of meriting a national emergency.

The very fact that national legislation was seldom implemented and that local schemes for the relief of the poor were seldom long-lasting is adequate testimony to the seriousness of the problem. It can be argued, correctly, that both local and national legislation, for at least much of the sixteenth century, failed because of municipal apathy, because of inadequate organisation: that, in any case, the philanthropy of most of the nation's wealthy – and not so wealthy – was sufficient to offset these deficiencies; but if the situation was as serious as was alleged by contemporaries and by later historians a state of anarchy would have prevailed in no time at all. It seems far more likely that the towns were adopting a temporary solution to a temporary problem and that this, as well as lack of money, at least partly explains the short-term nature of so many urban schemes. Governmental action was similarly short-term, even if repeated at intervals, and was intended to deal with existing situations. It is hardly likely that the Privy Council, which kept such a close watch on the situation, would have allowed the question of vagrancy to get out of hand, and Hext made it clear that some of the J.P.s, at least, were not prepared to watch a declining situation with complete equanimity. Norwich showed what could be done at short notice with only the threat of an emergency, and at the turn of the century the single parish of St Peter Mancroft – admittedly a large and wealthy one – was still gathering more than £100 a year from its inhabitants for the relief of the poor, and supporting the destitute of three other parishes as well as its own [**doc. 20**].

The conditions depicted by F. G. Emmison in Bedfordshire and Essex present a far truer picture of the normal situation than the chaos in Somerset described so vividly by Hext. Edward Hext was a genuine observer. He saw a situation which frightened him, and his fear still animates his letter to Burghley [**doc. 7**]. If the situation he described was typical and general then vagrancy was really a serious problem. But he was writing in unusual circumstances, in a period not only of national but of European famine. It is hardly surprising that he heard people say that they would not starve: it is not in the least surprising that a cartload of cheese was robbed, that grain shipments were attacked and that people sought to preserve their lives. This was not a normal situation, however. One suspects, too, that sheep and cattle stealing by professional vagrants, while undoubtedly occurring, was seldom of serious proportions except when food was really short.

The cities were filled with poor, but they normally led passive, if unpleasant, lives. Rogues existed in Tudor times, as they do today; unemployment, on occasion, was rife; but both were accepted as part of the seamier side of life. The unemployed, whether rogues or otherwise, were deemed prospectively dangerous, and the authorities, both national and local, took action accordingly. Ultimately, after considerable experiment, it was accepted that responsibility must be taken for both the impotent and the unemployed poor, but the numbers regularly supported rarely exceeded 4 or 5 per cent of the population. Those that were supported were absolutely destitute. Many who might have joined them were bolstered by the charitable bequests of all classes of society, and more than one tradesman was able to take advantage of the loan funds set up by his wealthier fellows. Merchant interest was paramount in this respect, and it would be over-cynical to assume that it stemmed entirely from belated pangs of conscience or from fears of social disturbance. Whatever the motive, it seems reasonably certain that the government was well in command of the situation. It was only in times of dire distress that the average working man reacted in a violent manner, and even then such violence was usually kept within reasonable bounds. In normal circumstances both poverty and vagrancy were fairly well contained, and to say that either created a dangerous national situation would be to strain the evidence.

Part Four: Documents

Causes of poverty

document 1

Problems of the Textile Trade

*Far more people were employed in textiles than in any other industry, with
the possible exception of agriculture. Many were completely dependent on the
trade and were, in consequence, especially hard hit in times of industrial
depression. It was found that whenever there was a falling off in demand:*

... infinite numbers of Spynners, Carders, Pickers of woll are
turned to begging with no smale store of pore children, who driven
with necessitie (that hath no lawe) both come idelie abowt to begg
to the oppression of the poore husbandmen, And robbe their hedges
of Lynnen, stele pig, gose, and capon, and leave not a drie hedg
within dyvers myles compas of the townes wher they dwell to the
great destruction of all mannor of grayen sowen and to the spoile
of mens meadowes and pastures, And spoile all springes, steale fruit
and corne in the harvest tyme, and robb barnes in the winter tyme,
and cawse pore maydes and servantes to purloyne and robbe their
masters, which the foresyd spynners etc. receve Besides many other
myscheifes falling owt the Weavers, Walkers, Tukkers, Shermen,
Dyers and suche being tall lusty men and extreame pore streyght
being forced by povertie stele fish conies, dere, and such like, and
their streight murmure and rayse comocions as late experience in
Suffolk shewed.

F. J. Fisher (**56**), quoting from Rawlinson MSS, D, 133, f.4b.

document 2

Enclosures

*Enclosure of common land is invariably discussed from the point of view of
the dispossessed, and those responsible subjected to universal criticism. It is
worth bearing in mind that some enclosure was both desirable and necessary,*

as the husbandman points out in this extract from A discourse of the Common Weal of this Realm of England.

Manie of vs saw, xij yere ago, that oure proffittes was but small by the plowes; and therefore divers of my neighboures that had in times past, some two, some thre, some fowre plowes of theire owne, have laid downe, some of them parte, and som of theym all theire teames, and turned ether part or all theire arable grounde into pasture, and thereby haue wexed verie Rich men. And everie day some of vs encloseth a plote of his ground to pasture; and weare it not that oure grounde lieth in the common feildes, intermingled one with a nother, I thincke also oure feildes had bene enclosed, of a common agreament of all the townshippe, longe ere this time. And to saie the truthe, I, that haue enclosed little or nothinge of my grownd, could never be able to make vp my lordes rent weare it not for a little brede of neate, shepe, swine, gese, and hens that I doe rere vpon my ground; whearof, because the price is sumwhat round, I make more cleare proffitt then I doe of all my corne; and yet I haue but a bare liuinge, by reason that manye thinges doe belonge to husbandrie which now be exceadinge chargeable, over they weare in times past.

E. Lamond, ed. (**21**), pp. 56–7.

document 3

Rack-renting

Bitter complaints were frequently made against men of noble and gentry stock who raised the rents of incoming tenants, and their action may have led, at least indirectly, to an increase in the number of the poor. Nevertheless, many had little alternative. Unless they were farming the demesne themselves, they had to combat ever rising prices with fixed incomes. Their tenants, in contrast, continued to pay the same rent while selling their surplus produce at enhanced prices. The knight, in this extract from A Discourse of the Common Weal, *defends the action taken by people of his class.*

Sir, I knowe it is true ye complayne not with oute a cause. So it is as true that I and my sorte, I meane all gentlemen, haue as greate, yea a far greater, cause to complayne then anie of youe haue; for as I sayed nowe that the price of thinges weare risen of all handes, youe may better live after youre degree then we, for youe may and doe raise the price of youre wares, as the price of victualles and other necessaries doo rise. And so can not we so muche; for thoughe it be true that of suche landes as come to oure handes, either by purchace or by determination and ending of suche termes of yeares or other estates that I or my auncestor had graunted thearin in times past, I doe either receive a better fyne then of old was vsed, or enhaunce the rent thereof, beinge forced thereto for the chardge of my howshold that is increased over that it was, yet in all my life time I looke not that the thirde parte of my lande shall come to my dispocition, that I maye enhaunce the rent of the same; but it shalbe in mens holdinges, either by lease or by copie, graunted before my time, and still contynuinge, and yet like to continewe in the same estate, for the most parte duringe my life, and perchaunce my sonnes; so as we can not rayse all our wares, as youe maye yours, and me thinkes yt weare reason we did. Any be reason we can not, so many of vs as haue departed . . . oute of the Countrie of late, haue bene driven to give over oure houshold, and to kepe either a chambere in London, or to waight on the courte vuncalled, with a man and a lacky after him, wheare he was wonte to kepe halfe a score cleane men in his house, and xx^{tie} or xxx^{tie} other persone besides, everie day in the weke.

E. Lamond, ed (**21**), pp. 19–20.

document 4

The loss of the monasteries

While the average amount of monastic charity may have been small, some houses were sufficiently generous to attract hordes of vagrants. It is at least possible that the existence of monasteries created far more vagrancy than their dissolution, especially in the more remote parts of the country. The Duke of Norfolk considered this to be so, as the following extract from a letter to Thomas Cromwell indicates.

2 June 1537. My veray goode Lorde . . . forasmoche as I do nowe wryght to the Kinges maiestie I shall not molest you with nothing conteyned in my lettre sent to his highnes. And where I do understand his maiestie hath now sent lettres to thiese parties concernyng vacabonds, your good lordship shall perceyve by copies of lettres which I have a good tyme past sent to all the justice of pease and religiouse houses in thies parties, that I haue not neglected that matier; surely I neuer sawe so many as be in thiese cuntrees. And the almes that they haue in religious houses is the great occasion

thereof, and also the slackenes of the Justice of pease, for not doying ther dewties. I haue and shall so order thiese cuntrees under my rewle that I thinke ye shall shortely here of no small nomber of them that shall drawe Southewards.

J. M. Clay, ed. (**9**), p. 48.

document 5

Diminishing hospitality

A number of people regarded the dissolution of the monasteries as a tragedy. Complaints were made particularly about the loss of hospitality, and monastic charity was compared favourably with that of the new owners of the estates, as these extracts show.

[a] For, although the sturdy beggers [the monks] gat all the deuotion of the good charitable people from them, yet had the pore impotent creatures some relefe of theyr scrappes, where as nowe they haue nothyng. Then had they hospitals, and almshouses to be lodged in, but nowe they lye and starue in the stretes. Then was ther number great, but nowe much greater.

'A supplication of the poore commons' (1546) from *Four Supplications*, Early English Text Society, p. 79.

[b] Again it was pitie the great lamentations that the poore people made for them [the monks], for there was great hospitalitie kept amonge them, and, as it was reported, tenne thousand persons had lost their living by the putting downe of theim, which was great pitie.

C. Wriothesley, *A Chronicle of England during the reigns of the Tudors*, Camden Society Publications, I, p. 43.

[c] But now that all the abbys, with ther londes, goodes, and impropred personages, be in temporal mennys handes, I do not heare tell that one halpenyworth of almes or any other profights cometh unto the peple of those parishes where such personagys be.

Brinklow, *Complaynt of Roderyk Mors*, Early English Text Society, p. 33.

The extent of poverty

An urban assessment

A census of Sheffield, taken in January 1615–16, indicates the extent of poverty in the town.

By a survaie of the towne of Sheffield made the second daye of Januarie 1615 by twenty foure of the most sufficient inhabitants there, it appearethe that there are in the towne of Sheffelde 2207 people; of which there are 725 which are not able to live without the charity of their neighbours. These are all begging poore. 100 householders which relieve others. These (though the best sorte) are but poor artificers; among them is not one which can keepe a teame on his own land, and not above tenn who have grounds of their own that will keepe a cow. 160 householders not able to relieve others. These are such (though they beg not) as are not able to abide the storme of one fortnights sickness but would be thereby driven to beggary. 1222 children and servants of the said householders; the greatest part of which are such as live of small wages, and are constrained to work sore to provide them necessaries.

Sidney and Beatrice Webb (**37**), pp. 82–3.

A rural assessment

Edward Hext, Justice of the Peace in Somerset, wrote to Burghley on 25 September 1596 concerning the increase of rogues and vagabonds. The letter is a key document on the situation in a crisis year, and shows the close link between local and central government.

Right honarable and my very good Lord,

Havynge long observed the rapynes and thefts Comytted within this Countye wher I serve, and fyndynge they multyplye daylye to the vtter impoverysshinge of the poore husbondman that beareth the greatest burthen of all services, And knowyng your most honorable Care of the preservacon of the peace of this land, [I] do thynck yt my bounden dewtye to present vnto your honorable and grave consideracion these Calenders inclosed of the prisoners executed and delyvered this yere past in this Countye of Somerset, wherein your Lordship may behold clxxxiij most wycked and desperate persons to be inlarged. And of these very fewe come to anye good, for none wyll receave them ynto servyce, And yn treuth worke they will not, nether canne they withowt most extreame paynes, by reason their zinowes are so benumed and styff throwghe Idlenesse as theyr lyms, beynge putt to any hard labor, wil greve them above measure, So as they will rather hazard ther lyves then work. And this I knowe to be trewe, for att suche tyme as our howses of Correccion weare vp (which are putt downe in most partes in Ingland, the more pyttye), I sent dyvers wandrynge suspycyous persons to the howse of Correccion, and all in generall wold beseche me wyth bytter teares to send them rather to the gayle, and denyinge yt them, some confessed felonyes vnto me by which they hazarded ther lyves, to thend they wold not be sent to the howse of Correccion, where they shold be ynforced to worke. Butt my good Lord, these are not all the theves and Robbers that are abroad in thys Countye, for I knowe that yn the experyens of my service heare, that the fyveth person that comytteth a felonye ys not browght to this tryall . . . yf they be [taken] and come ynto the hands of the symple man that hath lost his goods and lett them slypp, because he will not be bound to give evidens at the assises to hys troble and chardge; others are delyvered to simple Constables and tythingmen that sometymes wylfullye other tymes negligently suffer them to escape; others are brawght before some Iustice that eyther wanteth experyence to examyn a Cunnynge thief, or wyll not take the paynes that owght to be taken yn siftyng him uppon every circumstance and presumpsyon. . . . In . . . default of Iustice manye wicked theves escape, for most comonly the simple Cuntryman and woman, lokynge no farther then ynto the losse of ther owne goods, are of opynyon that they wold not procure a mans death for all the goods yn the world . . . And these that thus escape ynfect great numbers, ymboldenynge them by ther escapes, some havynge ther books by intreatye of the Iustices them selves that cannot reade a word, others havinge byn burnt in the hand more tymes than ones, for after a moneth or too ther wilbe no signe in the worlde. . . . And the greatest parte are nowe growen to thes petytt felonyes for which they may have ther booke, by which they are imboldened to this great wickednesse. And happy weare yt for England yf Clergy weare taken awaye in case of felonye.

... I do not see howe yt ys possible for the poore Cuntryman to bear the burthens dewly layde uppon hym ... there be [some] that styck not to say boldlye they must not starve, they wyll not starve. And this yere there assembled lxxx in a Companye and tooke a whole Carte loade of Cheese from one dryvynge yt to a fayre and dispersed yt amongest them, for which some of them have indured longe imprisonment and fyne by the Iudgement of the good Lord Chief Iustice att owr last Crisman Sessions, which may grow dangerous by the ayde of suche numbers as are abroade, especyally in this tyme of dearthe ... [they say] that the ritche men have gotten all into her handes and wyll starve the poore. And I may Iustlye saye that the Infynyte numbers of the Idle wandrynge people and robbers of the land are the chefest cause of the dearthe, for thowghe they labor not, and yet they spend dobly as myche as the laborer dothe, for they lye Idlely in the ale howses daye and nyght eatinge and drynkynge excessively. And within these iij monethes i tooke a thief that was executed this last assizes, that confessed vnto me that he and too more laye in an Alehouse three weeks, in which tyme they eate xx^{ti} fatt sheepe whereof they stole every night on, besydes they breake many a poore mans plowghe by stealing an oxe or too from him, and not beinge able to buy more leaseth a great parte of hys tyllage that yere, others leese ther shepe owte of ther folds, by which ther grounds are not so frutefull as otherwyse they wold be. ...

And when these lewde people are comytted to the gayle, the poore Cuntry that ys robbed by them are inforced there to feede them, which they greve att. And this yere ther hath bynne disbursed to the releefe of the prisoners in the gayle above lxxiij li, And yet they are alowed but vi^d a man weekely. ... Of wandrynge souldiers ther are more abroade than ever weare, notwithstanding her Maiesties most graycyous proclamacion lately sett forth for the suppressinge of them, which hathe not donne that good yt wold, yf yt had bynne vsed as yt owght, for the Iustices in every shere ... owght to have ... aquaynted all inferior officers with yt ... but the proclamacions beinge sent to the Shiryffs, they delyver them over to the Baylyffs to be proclaymed in the marketts; ther a fewe ignorant persons heares a thinge redd which they have lyttle to do with and lesse regard, and the xth Iustyce knoweth not yet that ever ther was any such proclamacion.

Your good Lordship may perceave by this Counterfect passe that I send you inclosed that the lewde yonge men of England ar devoted to this wicked course of lief, for the man that traveled by color of yt ys inheritor to xl li land after his father . . . a genthelman [who] dwelleth att northlache in the County of Gloucester. . . .

[The most] daungerous [are] the wandrying Souldiers and other stout roages of England . . . of these sort of wandrynge Idell people there ar three or fower hundred in a shere, and thowgh they goo by too and three in a Companye, yet all or the moste parte yn a shere do meete eyther att feare or markett, or in some Alehowse once a weeke. And yn a great haye howse in a remote place ther dyd resort weekely xl, sometymes lx, where they dyd roast all kynde of good meat. The inhabitants . . . made complaynte at our last Easter Sessions . . . wheruppon precepts weare made to the Counstables of the hundred, but fewe apprehended, for they have intellygens of all things intended agaynst them, for ther be of them that wilbe present at every assize, Sessions, and assembly of Iustices, and will so cloathe them selves for that tyme as anye shold deame him to be an honest husbondman, So as nothinge is spoken, donne, or intended to be donne but they knowe yt. I know this to be tru by the confession of some.

And they grow the more daungerous in that they fynde they have bread that feare in Iustices and other inferior officers that no man dares to call them into questyon. At a late sessions, a tall man, a verye sturdy and auncyent traveller, was Comytted by a Iustice and browght to the Sessions and had Iudgment to be whipped, he presently at the barre, in the face and hearynge of the whole benche, sware a great othe that yf he weare whipped yt should be the dearest whipping to some that ever was; yt strake suche a feare in him that Comytted him as he prayed he myght be deferred vntil the assises, wher he was delyvered without anye whipping or other harme, And the Iustice glad he had so pacyfyed his wrath . . . knowinge the danger that may growe by these wycked people to my dread and most deare soveraygnes most peaceable government, I will not leave yt unadvertysed, thowghe I shold hazard my lyef by yt. . . . from my poore howse att Netherham in Somersetshire this xxv[th] of September.

your good Lordships in all humbleness to be Comaunded,

Edw. Hext

R. H. Tawney and E. Power, eds. (**33**), ii, 339–46.

Types of vagrant

A contemporary description of a rogue

Harman, in his Caveat for Commen Cursetors, *published in 1567, lists no fewer than twenty-four different types of vagrant. The men and women referred to in the following documents are typical of many of their class.*

A rogue is known to all men by his name, but not to all men by his conditions: no puritan can dissemble more than he, for he will speak in a lamentable tune and crawl along the streets, (supporting his body by a staff) as if there were not life enough in him to put strength into his legs: his head shall be bound about with linen, loathsome to behold; and as filthy in colour as the complexion of his face; his apparel is all tattered, his bosom naked, and most commonly no shirt on: not that they are driven to this misery by mere want, but that if they had better clothes given them, they would rather sell them to some of their own fraternity than wear them, and wander up and down in that piteous manner, only to move people to compassion, and to be relieved with money, which being gotten, at night is spent as merrily and as lewdly as in the day it was won by counterfeit villainy. Another sect there be of these, and they are called STURDY ROGUES: these walk from county to county under colour of travelling to their friends or to find out some kinsman, or else to deliver a letter to one gentleman or other, whose name he will have fairly endorsed on paper folded up for that purpose, and handsomely sealed: others use this shift to carry a Certificate or passport about them, with the hand or seal of some Justice to it, . . . all these writings are but counterfeit, they having amongst them (of their own RANK), that can write and read, who are their secretaries in this business.

Thomas Dekker, *Bell-Man of London: A Discovery of all the idle Vaga-bonds in England: their Conditions: their laws amongst themselves: their degrees and orders: their meetings, and their manners of living, (both men and women)*, London, 1608, quoted by P. J. Helm, *England under the York-ists and Tudors, 1471–1603*, Bell, 1968.

document 9

A bawdy basket

These Bawdy Baskets be also wemen, and go with baskets and Capcases on their armes, wherein they haue laces, pynnes, nedles, white ynkell, and round sylke gyrdles of al colours. These wyl bye conneyskins, and steale linen clothes of on hedges. And for their trifles they will procure of mayden seruants, when their mystres or dame is oute of the waye, either some good peace of beefe, baken, or cheese, that shalbe worth xii pens, for ii pens of their toyes. . . . The vpright men haue good acquayntance with these, and will helpe and relieue them when they want. Thus they trade their lyues in lewed lothsome lechery.

R. H. Tawney and E. Power, eds. (**33**), iii, 414–15.

document 10

An Elizabethan Fagin

Some of the rogues inhabiting the Elizabethan underworld came from well-to-do backgrounds. The one referred to below was taken into custody by William Fleetwood, the indefatigable Recorder of London. Fleetwood's description of him, contained in a letter to Burghley, is reminiscent of Charles Dickens's Fagin.

Amongst our travels this one matter tumbled out of the way, that one Wotton, a gentleman-born and sometime a merchant-man of good credit, who falling by time into decay kept an ale-house at Smart's Quay near Billingsgate, and after that, for some misdemeanour being put down, he reared up a new kind of life, and in the same house he procured all the cutpurses about this city to repair to his said house. There was a school-house set up to learn young boys to cut purses. There were hung up two devices; the one was a pocket, the other a purse. The pocket had in it certain counters and was hung about with hawks' bells and over the top did hang a little sacring-bell; and he that could take out a counter without any noise was allowed to be a public foister; and he that could take a piece of silver out of the purse without the noise of any of the bells, he was adjudged a judicial nipper. . . . *Nota* that a foister is a pickpocket and a nipper is termed a pickpurse or cutpurse.

R. H. Tawney and E. Power, eds. (**33**), ii, 337–9.

document 11

Crime pays

Many beggars did extremely well out of their chosen profession. There is nothing to suggest that the woman named in this extract was anything out of the ordinary, yet the amount she had amassed from her begging operations was far greater than most labourers could ever hope to achieve. The total amount was £44 3s. 5d.

This daye was brought into the Courte certeyne money of one Mother Arden who used daly to go a beggying the strettes, viz., in olde grotes xxix^{li}xiii^{s}iiii^d; too olde angelles; in slypper vi^{li}xiii^{s}vi^d; more in slypper lxiii^s; and in new mony lxxiii^{s}vii^d. And there was taken owte and delyvered to Mother Arden vi^{s}viii^d of the foresayde sume.

Norwich Corporation Court Books, 1562–1569, folio 29. The entry was among those dated 12 September 1562.

The Norwich census

document 12

Poor families in Norwich

*This extract from the census of the Norwich poor gives an impression of normal poor families as distinct from the professional vagrants. The census survives in its entirety, and is unique both in the amount of detail given of people of this class and in the number of families recorded. It is transcribed in its entirety, with an analytical introduction, in J. F. Pound ed. (**98**). A much smaller census of the Ipswich poor, with less detail than that of the Norwich one, is printed in Webb (**36**).*

ST. STEVENS P(A)RRYSHE (AND WARD)

Robert Rowe of 46 yers, glasier, in no worke, & Elizabeth, his wyfe, that spyn white warp; & 5 children, 2 sons, the eldest 16 yeris that kepe children, & the rest the daughters spyn, & hav dwelt here ever. (hable) – Thomas Masons house. No allms. Indeferent.

Agnes Nicols, wedow, of 40 yere, that sowe & have dwelt here ever. (hable) – Thomas Browns house. No alms. Indeferent.

John Hubberd of 38 yere, bocher & occupi slawteri, & Margaret, his wyfe, of 30 yer that sell souce etc., & 2 yonge children, & hav dwelt here ever. (hable) No alms. Veri pore.

Ane Bucke, wedow, of 46 yeris, a souster & teacher of children, & 2 children of 9 & 5 yer & work lace, & have dwelt here ever (hable) No alms. Veri pore.

Richard Gugle of 30 yer, glaser, that work not, & Dorethe, his wyf, of that age that spyn white warp, & a yonge child, & dwelt her ever. (hable) – His owne house. Indeferent.

Margaret Turn(er), wedow, of 50 yer, that spyn & help others, & hav dwelt her 12 yer (hable) – Ro. Carters house. Indeferent.

Johane Bongey, wedowe, of 60 yere, that spyn white warp & have dwelt here ever. No allms. Veri pore.

& Elizabeth Norton of 40 yere that spyn & help other (hable) (At Osmondes) Veri pore.

Wylliam Carter (at Carters) of 22 yer that is dyseased of a sore legge, & withoute comforte, & hath dwelt here ever (hable) No alms. Veri pore.

Thomas Pele of 50 yere, a cobler in worke, & Margaret, his wyfe, that spyn white warp; & 3 children, theldest 16 yere & spin, & thother 2, 12 & 6 yere, & go to skole & hav dwelt her 9 yere & cam oute of Yorkshire. (hable) – The paryshe house. No alms. Veri pore.

Robert Galiarde of 60 yer, laborer in no worke, & Margaret, his wyfe, of that age, that spyn white warpe (hable) – The parryshe house. No alms. Indeferent.

& Elizabeth Gray, wydow, of 36 yers, that spyn also, & hath a son of 4 yers, & hav dwelt here 5 yers, & cam from Wrouxham (hable). No alms. Veri pore.

J. F. Pound ed., *The Norwich Census of the Poor, 1570*, Norfolk Record Society, Vol. XL, 1971, p. 43. St Stephen's had a further 39 families recorded.

document 13

A poor man's property

The following inventory gives an impression of a poor man's possessions at the end of the sixteenth century. The labourer concerned was more fortunate than most, for he did at least have some property to leave.

A true and perfect inventorye of all and singuler the goods and chattells of Thomas Herries late deceased in the parishe of St.

Gregoryes in Norwich prysed by us William Rogers and Gregorye
Wesbye the xvth daye of October in the yeare of our Lord God 1599

In primis:	one borded bedsted	3s. 4d.
Item:	one mattresse and one under cloathe	1s. 6d.
Item:	one flocke bed	2s. 6d.
Item:	one bolster	2s. 0d.
Item:	one downe pillowe and an old cushaigne	1s. 6d.
Item:	two leather pillowes filled with feathers	3s. 4d.
Item:	one payer of shetes	2s. 0d.
Item:	one bed blanket	1s. 8d.
Item:	one old cofer	2s. 0d.
Item:	one drye barrell	3d.
Item:	2 salt boxes	1s. 0d.
Item:	one hake, a fyer pann, a payer of tonges and a rostinge yron	1s. 6d.
Item:	one litle ketle, a sawer and 3 pewter spoones	2s. 6d.
Item:	3 little boles	1s. 0d.
Item:	one ketle, one potspone, 28 trenyens	1s. 0d.
Item:	2 woodinge platters and 5 dishes and twoo erthen potts	8d.
Item:	a stone pott and 5 galley pottes	4d.
Item:	a hamper and certen old washe	6d.
Item:	4 frayles and 2 stooles	6d.
Item:	a little table and 4 stoles	3s. 0d.
Item:	3 chiselles, 2 hamers and a perser	8d.
Item:	3 old cushings	6d.
Item:	2 payers of hand cuffes and one dozen of hand kerchers and an old pillowbere	2s. 6d.
Item:	2 old shirtes	1s. 8d.
Item:	one old forme and 2 old cappes	1s. 0d.
Total:		£1 18s. 5d.

[The sums of money were given in Roman numerals in the original
inventory]

J. F. Pound (**74**) p. 121.

Legislation

Repression

Until 1576 the government made no distinction between the professional beggar and the unemployed man who would have preferred to work. Any fit person who had neither occupation nor income was liable to be subjected to the treatment referred to below. The extracts are from the Act of 1531.

. . . and be it further enacted . . . that if any man or woman being whole and mighty in body and able to labour having no land, master, nor using any lawful merchandise, craft, or mystery, whereby he might get his living . . . be vagrant and can give none reckoning how he doth lawfully get his living, that then it shall be lawful to the constables and all the King's officers, ministers, and subjects of every town, parish, and hamlet, to arrest the said vagabonds and idle persons and to bring them to any of the Justices of Peace of the same shire or liberty . . . and that every such Justice of Peace . . . shall cause every such idle person so to him brought to be had to the next market town or other place where the said Justices of Peace . . . shall think most convenient . . . and there to be tied to the end of a cart naked and be beaten with whips throughout the same market town or other place till his body be bloody by reason of such whipping; and after such punishment and whipping had, the person so punished . . . shall be enjoined upon his oath to return forthwith without delay in the next and straight way to the place where he was born, or where he last dwelled before the same punishment by the space of three years, and there put himself to labour like as a true man oweth to do.

Statutes of the Realm, iii, 328.

A compulsory poor rate

After several attempts at persuasion, the government followed the example of London and Norwich and introduced a compulsory poor rate in 1572.

. . . And when the number of the said poor people forced to live upon alms be by that means truly known, the said justices, mayors, sheriffs, bailiffs, and other officers shall within like convenient time devise and appoint, within every their said several divisions, meet and convenient places by their discretions to settle the same poor people for their habitations and abidings, if the parish within the which they shall be found shall not or will not provide for them; and shall also within like convenient time number all the said poor people within their said several limits, and thereupon (having regard to the number) set down what portion the weekly charge towards the relief and sustenation of the said poor people will amount to within every their said several divisions and limits; and that done, they ... shall by their good discretions tax and assess all and every the inhabitants, dwelling in all and every city, borough, town, village, hamlet and place known within the said limits and divisions, to such weekly charge as they and every of them shall weekly contribute towards the relief of the said poor people, and the names of all such inhabitants taxed shall also enter into the said register book together with their taxation ... and also shall appoint the overseers of the said poor people by their discretions, to continue also for one whole year; and if they do refuse to be overseers, then every of them so refusing to forfeit ten shillings for every such default.

Statutes of the Realm, iv pt i, 590–8.

document 16

The unemployed set to work

The Act of 1576 introduced the new principle of setting the unemployed to work on stocks supplied or public works.

... Also to the intent youth may be accustomed and brought up in labour and work, and thus not like to grow to be idle rogues, and to the intent also that such as be already grown up in idleness and so [be] rogues at this present, may not have any just excuse in saying that they cannot get any service or work, and then without any favour or toleration worthy to be executed, and that other poor and needy persons being willing to work may be set on work: be it ordered and enacted by the authority aforesaid, that in every city and town corporate within this realm, a competent store and stock of wool, hemp, flax, iron or other stuff, by the appointment and order of the mayor, bailiffs, justices or other head officers having rule in the said cities or towns corporate (of themselves and all others the inhabitants within their several authorities to be taxed, levied and gathered), shall be provided . . . Collectors and governors of the poor from time to time (as cause requireth) shall and may, of the same stock and store, deliver to such poor and needy persons a competent portion to be wrought into yarn or other matter within such time and in such sort as in discretions shall be from time to time limited and prefixed, and the same afterwards, being wrought, to be from time to time delivered to the said collectors and governors of the poor, for which they shall make payment to them which work the same according to the desert of the work, and of new deliver more to be wrought; and so from time to time to deliver stuff unwrought and receive the same again wrought as often as cause shall require; which hemp, wool, flax, or other stuff wrought from time to time, shall be sold by the said collectors and governors of the poor either at some market or other place, and at such time as they shall think meet, and with the money coming of the sale, to buy more stuff in such wise as the stocks or store shall not be decayed in value.

Statutes of the Realm, iv pt i, 610–13.

document 17

The Poor Law Act of 1601

By the end of the sixteenth century it was accepted that provision had to be made for all categories of poor. The extract below gives an impression of the all-embracing nature of the Act of 1601.

Be it enacted by the authority of this present parliament, that the churchwardens of every parish, and four, three, or two substantial householders there as shall be thought meet, having respect to the apportion and greatness of the same parish or parishes, to be nominated yearly in Easter week or within one month after Easter, under the hand and seal of two or more justices of the peace in the same county, whereof one to be of the quorum, dwelling in or near the same parish or division where the same parish doth lie, shall be called overseers of the poor of the same parish: and they or the greater part of them shall take order from time to time, by and with the consent of two or more justices of peace as is aforesaid, for setting to work of the children of all such whose parents shall not by the said churchwardens and overseers . . . be thought able to keep and maintain their children; and also for setting to work all such persons married or unmarried having no means to maintain them, [or] use no ordinary or daily trade of life to get their living by; and also to raise weekly or otherwise, by taxation of every inhabitant parson, vicar and other, and of every occupier of lands, houses, tithes impropriate or propriations of tithes, coal mines or saleable underwoods, in the said parish, in such competent sum or sums of money as they shall think fit, a convenient stock of flax, hemp, wool, thread, iron and other necessary ware and stuff to set the poor on work, and also competent sums of money for and towards the necessary relief of the lame, impotent, old, blind, and such other among them being poor and not able to work, and also for the putting out of such children to be apprentices, to be gathered out of the same parish; . . . which said churchwardens and overseers so to be nominated, or such of them as shall not be let by sickness or other just excuse to be allowed by two such justices of peace or more as aforesaid, shall meet together at the least once every month in the church of the said parish, upon the Sunday in the afternoon after Divine Service, there to consider of some good course to be taken and of some meet order to be set down in the premises, and shall within four days after the end of their year and after overseers nominated as aforesaid, make and yield up to such two justices of peace as is aforesaid a true and perfect account of all sums of money by them received, and also of such stock as shall be in their hands or in the hands of any of the poor to work, and of all other things concerning their said office; and such sum or sums of money as shall be in their hands shall pay and deliver over to the said churchwardens and overseers newly nominated and appointed as aforesaid. . . .

And be it further enacted that it shall be lawful for the said churchwardens and overseers, or the greater part of them, by the assent of any two justices of the peace aforesaid, to bind any such children as aforesaid to be apprentices, where they shall see convenient, till such man-child shall come to the age of four and twenty years, and such woman-child to the age of one and twenty years, or the time of her marriage; the same to be as effectual to all purposes as if such child were of full age, and by indenture of covenant bound him or herself.

And the said justices of peace or any of them to send to the house of correction or common gaol such as shall not employ themselves to work, being appointed thereunto as aforesaid.

Statutes of the Realm, vol. iv, pt ii, 962–5.

Local schemes of poor relief

The first compulsory poor rate

Document 18

The first compulsory poor rate was levied in London in 1547.

For Asmoche as the late order Lately Deuysed and taken by the Lorde Maire and Aldermen for the Releiff, mayntenaunce and fyndyng of the poore, Sicke and indigent persones Apoynted to be founde and kepte within the house and hospytall Lately erectyd and founded by the most noble prynce of famous memorye King Henry the eight, As well at the costes and charges of the Citezeins and inhabitantes of this Citie as of the proffitz and Reuenues of Such Londes and tenementes as his highnesse indowyd the same house withall, by the Deuocyon and Charitable Almes of the people wekely to be gatheryd within the parrisshe chjrches of the said Citie Dothe not take eny good Successe or Semblans of good contynu-ance, Yt ys therefore for Remedye and Supportacion thereof this Daye by the lorde maire, Aldermen and commens in this present Commen Councell assemblyd and by auctoritie of the same Ordeyned, enactyd, grauntyd and establysshed that the Citezeins and inhabitantes of the said Citie Shall Furthwith Contrybute and paye towardes the Sustentacyon, maynteynyng and fyndyng of the said poore personages by the space of one hole yere now next ensuyng the moitie or half deale of one hole fiftene, And that the said wekely colleccyon of the Deuocyon of the people for that entent and purpose shall from henceforthe vtterly Ceasse and be Discharged. . . . And yt ys also enacted and Agreyd by the said Auctoritie that yt shalbe liefull for all and euery the petye collec-tours of the said Moytie or half deale of the said xv^{ne} to distrayne all and euery persone and persones that shall Refuse or denye to Content and paye all Suche Summe and Summes of Money as he or they Shalbe assessed at towardes the Said Payment.

Guildhall Journal, xv, f. 325b, 1547.

The Norwich scheme

document 19

The following extract from the Norwich orders for the poor gives the official reasons for the inauguration of the city's scheme. The fact that fewer than *thirty beggars were arrested in Norwich in each of the preceding two years suggests that the rising of 1570 (**71**), which was originally intended to link up with that of the Northern Earls, may have been a decisive factor. Certainly, Cecil's letter to the mayor in that year made specific reference to vagrants and the state of the poor. (**98**, p. 9). Beggars had aided Ket's rebels in 1549, a factor which may have contributed to the inauguration of a compulsory poor rate about the same time, and even the threat of insurrection could not be ignored.*

This book and orders made within the Cittye of Norwiche had manye occasions moved thereunto for the better provision of the poore, the ponishement of vacabondes, the settinge on worke of loyterers and other idle parsons, thexpulcinge of stronge beggers, the mayntayninge the indigente and nedie, and the practizinge of youthe to be trayned in worke, in learninge and in the feare of God, so as no parson shoulde have neede to goe abegginge nor be suffred to begge within the seyde cittye. . . .

Fyrste for that dyverse of the cittizens felte themselves agreeved that the cittie was so replenysshed with greate nombres, poore people, bothe men, women and chyldren, to the nombre of ij^m and ccc parsons whoe for the moste parte wente dayely abroade from dore to dore counterfeattinge a kinde of worke but indeede dyd verie lyttle or none at all.

And for that they were soffred and nourished at everied mans dore withoute inqueringe from wheare they came, they encreased to suche noombre as the strangers beggars (onelye) surcharges the cittie above cc poundes by yere.

Moreover those that daielie wente abowt pretendinge to satisfye their hunger, were not onelye contented to take at mens doores that suffized them, but being overgorged they caste foorthe the reste into the streete, so that they might be followed by the sight thereof in pottage, breade, meate, and drinke which they spoiled verie voluptuouslye.

Agayne, these crewes in their contynual beggynge respected no worke to prepare them lodginge, but used churche porshes, mens seller[s], doores, barnes and haye chambers, and other back corners to bestowe themselves, and suche as had howses did not worke for lodginge other then that they laye upon the colde grownde. So cared they not for apparell, though the colde strooke so deepe into them, that what with diseases and wante of shyftenge their Fleshe was eaton with vermyne and corrupte diseases grew upon them so faste and so grevouslye as they were paste remedye, and so much charges (by this meanes) bestowed upon one that wold have suffized a great sorte came all to waste and consummacion, nott with standinge their churche gatheringe (some tyme twoo or thre in a daye) so greved the inhabitantes that theye ernestly called for reformacion, aludinge [alleging] the common colleccion, the charges at their doores to be verie excessive.

More over, for wante of brewers and lookers abowte, the victualling houses were stuffed with players and dronkerdes that so tended the drynke all daye that they could not enclyne to woorke. And in ther pottes they abused the holy name of God with swearenge, pratinge and lyenge to the gret offence of all mightye God, the distruccion of them selves and the common wealthe, defiled ther bodies with filthiness that the ofte ponnishinge their vices so occupied the maiestrates as the chief matters of the comon wealthe was fayne to be delayede, that other wayes had moste nede of precedinge, although dives skaped unponnisshed.

R. H. Tawney and E. Power, eds. (**33**), ii, 316–17.

The role of the parish **document 20**

This extract from the accounts of the overseers of the poor of St Peter Mancroft, Norwich, for the year 1598–99 shows how important parish rates were for the relief of the destitute. It required a large and wealthy parish to collect more than £100 a year from its inhabitants for this purpose, but very many smaller districts, both rural and urban, were contributing in the same way.

The accounte of John Tesmond, Wm Peter, Wm Drake & Lionel Claxton, overseers for the pore of ye parish of St Peter of Mancroft appointed at ye feast of Easter anno Rne Elizabeth xl & of John Quashe & Richard Rosse churchwardens of the parish afforesayd according to the fourme of the statute in that cases provided, made & yelded up to the Justice of the peace of the citty of Norwich & to the new overseers & churchwardens for the parish aforesaid now newly appointed, the xiii day of Aprill anno domini 1599 as followeth vid

In primis collected by the assessment booke	107li	12s	8d
Item collected for ye shambles & stales	2	11	8
Summa totalis rec.	110	4	4

Paymentes	li	s	d
In primis: payde to the pore within the parish of St Peters according to ye wekely sessment	56	3	10
Item: payde in relief of them in extremety of sickness	2	7	3
Item: Payde for ye keping of ij of Bradleys children	3	—	—
Item: Payde for ye keping & putting out of Kindlemarsh his childe to be apprentice	3	—	—

	li	s	d
Item: payde for keping of Clarkes childe		18	4
Item: payde for keping of Danielles childe		13	6
Item: payd for ye nursing of a yong infant left in the parish one weke		1	8
Item: payd to goodwif Vowte for keping of iij children left in the parish		10	0
Item: payd for putting out of Thomas Clarke to be an apprentice		9	1
Item: payd for appeling & putting out of a vagrant bastard borne in ye parish	2	11	4
Item: paide to ye cunstables for sending away of vagabounds		4	8
Item: payde for ye keping of a poisened man in the tyme of his sicknes	1	13	8
Item: payd for putting of him to ye spittlehouse		10	0
Item: payd to ye collectors of St. John	24	8	0
Item: payd to the overseers of St. Myhelles	12	5	0
Item: paid to ye overseers of St. Giles		8	0
Sum totalis	110	4	4

Reproduced by kind permission of the Vicar of St Peter Mancroft. The accounts cover the years 1599 to 1636, and are in a book entitled *St Stephen's Parish*, 1812, although the contents have nothing to do with that parish or with the nineteenth century.

Bibliography

PRIMARY SOURCES

A great deal of material concerning vagrancy, in particular, is to be found in *Letters and Papers of Henry VIII* and, to an even greater extent, in the *Calendar of State Papers Domestic* for the reigns of Edward VI, Mary I and Elizabeth I. Where poverty is concerned, the information available varies from area to area. Most County Record Offices have at least some Court Books, Quarter Sessions Records and, where appropriate, account books and other details of Houses of Correction and hospitals which were instituted for the relief of the poor. Some, such as Ipswich and Norwich, have original censuses of the poor, as well as very full details of the poor law schemes set up by the local authorities. In rural areas, information is derived almost entirely from the accounts of the churchwardens and overseers of the poor. Much of this material is still buried in parish chests throughout the country. In a county such as Norfolk, which has been thoroughly investigated by the Reverend Folland and his helpers, considerable additional information has come to light, and it is to be hoped that their example will be followed elsewhere.

Where material of this sort is in print, details are normally to be found in Conyers Read's *Bibliography of British History in the Tudor Period*, London, 1959.

SECONDARY SOURCES

1 Ashley, W. J., *An Introduction to English Economic History and Theory*, Longman, 1892.
2 Aydelotte, Frank, *Elizabethan Rogues and Vagabonds*, Oxford University Press, 1913.
3 Bagley, J. J., *The English Poor Law*, Macmillan, Sources of History series, 1966.
4 Beresford, M. W., *The Lost Villages of England*, Lutterworth Press, 1954.
5 Bland, A. E., Brown, P. A. and Tawney, R. H. (eds), *English Economic History: Select Documents*, Bell, 1914.

6 Campbell, Mildred, *The English Yeoman under Elizabeth and the Early Stuarts*, Yale University Press, 1946; Merlin Press, 1960.

7 Cheyney, E. P., *A History of England from the defeat of the Armada to the death of Elizabeth*, New York, Peter Smith, 1948, 2 vols.

8 Clapham, Sir J. A., *A Concise Economic History of Britain from the Earliest Times to 1750*. Cambridge University Press, 1949.

9 Clay, J. M., *Yorkshire Monasteries: Suppression Papers*, Yorks. Archaeological Society Records Series, xlviii, 1912.

10 Dickens, A. G., *The English Reformation*, Batsford, 1964.

11 Dodd, A. H., *Life in Elizabethan England*, Batsford, 1960.

12 Eden, F. M., *The State of the Poor*, London, 1797, 3 vols.

13 Elton, G. R., *The Tudor Constitution*, Cambridge University Press, 2nd ed. 1982.

14 Fletcher, Anthony, *Tudor Rebellions*, Longman (Seminar Studies in History), 3rd ed. 1983.

15 Furnivall, F. J., ed. *The Rogues and Vagabonds of Shakespeare's Youth*, New Shakespeare Society, 6th Series, vii, 1880.

16 Hill, J. E. C., *Society and Puritanism in Pre-Revolutionary England*, Secker & Warburg, 1964.

17 Hudson, W. and Tingey, J. C., *The Records of Norwich*, Norwich, 1910, 2 vols.

18 Jordan, W. K., *Philanthropy in England*, Allen & Unwin, 1959.

19 Jordan, W. K., *The Rural Charities of England*, Allen & Unwin, 1961.

20 Judges, A. V., ed. *The Elizabethan Underworld*, Routledge, 1965.

21 Lamond, E., ed. *A Discourse of the Common Weal of this Realm of England* (1893), Cambridge University Press, reprinted 1929, 1954.

22 Leonard, E. M., *The Early History of English Poor Relief*, Cambridge University Press, 1900.

23 MacCaffrey, W. T, *Exeter, 1540–1640*, Harvard University Press, 1958.

24 More, Sir Thomas, *The Utopia of Sir Thomas More*, ed. J. H. Lupton, Oxford University Press, 1895.

25 Neale, Sir John, *Elizabeth and her Parliaments*, Cape, 1953, 2 vols.

26 Ramsey, P., *Tudor Economic Problems*, Gollancz, 1963.

27 Ribton-Turner, C. J., *A History of Vagrants and Vagrancy and Beggars and Begging*, London, 1887.

28 Rowse, A. L., *The England of Elizabeth*, Macmillan, 1950.

29   Savine, A., *English Monasteries on the eve of the Dissolution*, Oxford Studies in Social and Legal History I, ed. P. Vinogradoff, 1909.

30   Steinbicker, C. R., *Poor Relief in the Sixteenth Century, Studia Facultas Theologica*, xlviii, Washington, 1937.

31   Stone, L., *The Crisis of the Aristocracy*, Clarendon Press, 1965.

32   Tawney, R. H., *The Agrarian Problem in the Sixteenth Century*. Longman, 1912.

33   Tawney, R. H., and Power, Eileen, eds. *Tudor Economic Documents*, London, 1924, 3 vols.

34   Thirsk, Joan, ed. *The Agrarian History of England and Wales*, iv, *1540–1640*, Cambridge University Press, 1967.

35   Ware, S. L., *The Elizabethan Parish in its Ecclesiastical and Financial Aspect*, Baltimore, 1908.

36   Webb, John, *Poor Relief in Elizabethan Ipswich*, Suffolk Records Society, vol. ix, 1966.

37   Webb, Sidney and Webb, Beatrice, *English Poor Law History, Part I, The Old Poor Law*, London, 1927.

38   Williams, C. H., *English Historical Documents*, vol. v, *1485–1558*, Eyre & Spottiswoode, 1967.

39   Williams, Penry, *Life in Tudor England*, Batsford, 1964.

40   Woodward, G. W. O., *The Dissolution of the Monasteries*, Blandford, 1966.

41   Wright, T., *Three Chapters of Letters relating to the Suppression of the Monasteries*, Camden Society, 1843.

ARTICLES AND PAMPHLETS

42   Beresford, M. W., 'Habitation versus improvement. The debate on enclosure by agreement', in *Essays in the Economic and Social History of Tudor and Stuart England*, ed. F. J. Fisher, Cambridge University Press, 1961.

43   Bindoff, S. T., *Kets Rebellion*, Historical Association Pamphlet, General Series, 12, 1949.

44   Brenner, Y. S., 'The inflation of prices in early sixteenth-century England', *Economic History Review*, 2nd series, xiv, 1961.

45   Brenner, Y. S., 'The inflation of prices in England, 1551–1660', *Economic History Review*, 2nd series, xv, 1962.

46   Brown, E. H. Phelps and Hopkins, Sheila V., 'Wage-rates and prices. Evidence for population pressure in the sixteenth century', *Economica*, new series, xxiv, 1957.

47 Brown, E. H. Phelps and Hopkins, Sheila V., 'Builders' wage-rates. Prices and population: some further evidence', *Economica*, new series, xxvi, 1959.

48 Charman, D., 'Wealth and trade in Leicester in the early sixteenth century', *Leicestershire Archaeological Society*, xxv, 1949.

49 Coleman, D. C., 'Labour in the English Economy of the Seventeenth Century', *Economic History Review*, 2nd series, viii, 1955–56.

50 Davies, C. S. L., 'Slavery and Protector Somerset; the Vagrancy Act of 1547', *Economic History Review*, 2nd series, xix, no. 3, Dec. 1966.

51 Dickens, A. G., 'Tudor York', in *Victoria County History of Yorkshire*, vol. iv, Oxford University Press, 1961.

52 Elton, G. R., 'An early Tudor poor law', *Economic History Review*, 2nd series, vi, 1953

53 Emmison, F. G., 'Poor-relief accounts of two rural parishes in Bedfordshire, 1563–98', *Economic History Review*, iii, 1931.

54 Emmison, F. G., 'The care of the poor in Elizabethan Essex', *Essex Review*, lxii, 1953.

55 Everitt, Alan, 'Farm labourers', ch. vii in Thirsk, *Agrarian History of England, 1540–1640* (**34**).

56 Fisher, F. J., 'Commercial trends and policy in sixteenth-century England', in *Essays in Economic History*, vol. i, ed. E. Carus-Wilson, Edward Arnold, 1966.

57 Gay, E. F., 'Inclosures in England in the sixteenth century', *Quarterly Journal of Economics*, xvii, 1903.

58 Gay, E. F., 'Inquisitions of Depopulation in 1517 and the Domesday of Inclosures', *Transactions of the Royal Historical Society*, new series, xiv, 1900.

59 Hill, J. E. C., 'The many headed monster in late Tudor and early Stuart political thinking', in *From the Renaissance to the Counter-Reformation*, ed. C. H. Carter, Cape, 1966.

60 Hoskins, W. G., 'English provincial towns in the early sixteenth century', *Transactions of the Royal Historical Society*, 5th series, vi, 1956.

61 Hoskins, W. G., 'An Elizabethan town – Leicester', in his *Provincial England*, Macmillan, 1963.

62 Hoskins, W. G., 'Harvest fluctuations and English economic History, 1480–1619', *Agricultural History Review*, xii, 1964.

63 Kerridge, Eric, 'Social and economic history, 1485–1660', in *Victoria County History of Leicestershire*, vol. iv, London, 1958.

64 Matthews, C. M., 'Annals of the poor: taken from the records of a Hertfordshire village', *History Today*, v, 1955.

65 Outhwaite, R. B., *Inflation in Tudor and early Stuart England*, Macmillan (Studies in Economic History), 1969.

66 Pound, J. F., 'An Elizabethan census of the poor', in *Birmingham University Historical Journal*, viii, 1962.

67 Pound, J. F., 'The social and trade structure of Norwich, 1525–1575', *Past and Present*, xxxii, July, 1966.

68 Thirsk, Joan, 'Industries in the countryside' in *Essays in the Economic and Social History of Tudor and Stuart England*, ed. F. J. Fisher, Cambridge University Press, 1961.

69 Thirsk, Joan, *Tudor Enclosures*, Historical Association Pamphlet G.41, 1959.

70 Unwin, George, 'Industries', in *Victoria County History of Suffolk*, vol. ii, London, 1907.

71 Williams, Neville, 'The risings in Norfolk, 1569–1570', *Norfolk Archaeology*, xxxii.

THESES

72 Anderson, Kitty, 'The treatment of vagrancy and the relief of the poor and destitute in the Tudor period, based upon the local records of London to 1552 and Hull to 1576', London PhD., 1933.

73 Hammond, R. J., 'The social and economic circumstances of Ket's Rebellion', London PhD., 1934.

74 Pound, J. F., 'The Elizabethan Corporation of Norwich, 1558–1603', Birmingham University M.A., 1962.

BOOK REVIEWS

75 Stone, Lawrence, Review of W. K. Jordan's *Philanthropy in England* (**18**) in *History*, 1959, pp. 257–60.

76 Wilson, Charles, Review of W. K. Jordan's *Philanthropy in England* (**18**) in *English Historical Review*, 1960, pp. 685–7.

UNPUBLISHED MATERIAL

77 Some of the statements in this book are based on the as yet unpublished research of the writer into the history of Norfolk and Suffolk.

Supplementary bibliography

BOOKS

78 Appleby, A. B., *Famine in Tudor and Stuart England*, Stanford University Press, 1978.

79 Beier, A. L., *The Problem of the Poor in Tudor and Early Stuart England*, Methuen, 1983.

80 Clark, P. and Slack, P., eds *Crisis and Order in English Towns 1500–1700*, Routledge, 1972.

81 Clark, P. and Slack, P., *English Towns in Transition 1500–1700*, Oxford University Press, 1976.

82 Clark, P., ed. *The Early Modern Town: A Reader*, Longman, 1976.

83 Clark, P., ed. *Country Towns in Pre-Industrial England*, Leicester University Press, 1981.

84 Cockburn, J. S., ed. *Crime in England 1550–1800*, Methuen, 1977.

85 Coleman, D. C., *The Economy of England 1450–1750*, Oxford University Press, 1977.

86 Dyer, A. D., *The City of Worcester in the Sixteenth Century*, Leicester University Press, 1973.

87 Gould, J. D., *The Great Debasement: Currency and the Economy in mid-Tudor England*, Oxford University Press, 1970.

88 Holderness, B. A., *Pre-industrial England: Economy and Society from 1500 to 1750*, Dent, 1976.

89 Hoskins, W. G. *The Age of Plunder: King Henry's England 1500–1547*, Longman, 1976.

90 Jones, W. R. D. *The mid-Tudor crisis 1539–1563*, Macmillan, 1973.

91 Loach, Jennifer and Tittler, Robert, eds *The mid-Tudor Polity, c. 1540–1560*, Macmillan, 1980.

92 Lis, C. and Soly, H., *Poverty and Capitalism in pre-industrial Europe*, Harvester Press, 1979.

93 Minchinton, W. E., *Wage Regulation in Pre-Industrial England*, David and Charles, 1972.

94 Open University, *English Urban History 1500–1780*: Block 3, The Fabric of the Traditional Community; Block 4, The Traditional Community under Stress.

95 Palliser, D. M., *Tudor York*, Oxford University Press, 1979.

96 Palliser, D. M., *The Age of Elizabeth: England under the later Tudors, 1547–1603*, Longman, 1983.

97 Phythian-Adams, C., *Desolation of a City: Coventry and the*

Urban Crisis of the Late Middle Ages, Cambridge University Press, 1979.

98 Pound, J. F., ed. *The Norwich Census of the Poor, 1570*, Norfolk Record Society, Vol. XL, 1971.

99 Ramsey, P. H., ed. *The Price Revolution in Sixteenth-Century England*, Methuen, 1971.

100 Salgado, G., *Cony Catchers and Bawdy Baskets*, Penguin, 1972.

101 Salgado, G., *The Elizabethan Underworld*, Dent, 1977.

102 Sharp, Buchanan *In Contempt of All Authority: Rural Artisans and Riot in the West of England, 1586–1660*, University of California, 1980.

103 Slack, P. *et al, The Plague Reconsidered: A New Look at Its Origins and Effects in Sixteenth and Seventeenth Century England*, Local Population Studies, 1977.

104 Thirsk, J., *Economic Policy and Projects: The Development of a Consumer Society in Early Modern England*, Clarendon Press, 1978.

105 Webster, C., ed. *Health, Medicine and Mortality in the Sixteenth Century*, Cambridge University Press, 1979.

106 Williams, Penry, *The Tudor Regime*, Oxford University Press, 1979.

107 Wrightson, K. and Levine, D., *Poverty and Piety in an English Village: Terling, 1525–1700*, Academic Press, 1979.

108 Wrigley, E. A. and Schofield, R. S., *The Population History of England, 1541–1871: A Reconstruction*, Edward Arnold, 1981.

ARTICLES

109 Appleby, A. B., 'Disease or Famine? Mortality in Cumberland and Westmorland, 1580–1640' *Economic History Review*, 2nd series xxvi, 1973.

110 Appleby, A. B., 'Common land and peasant unrest in Sixteenth-century England: A Comparative Note', *Peasant Studies Newsletter*, iv, 3, July 1975.

111 Appleby, A. B., 'Nutrition and disease: the case of London, 1550–1750', *Journal of Interdisciplinary History*, vi, 1975–6.

112 Appleby, A. B., 'Grain Prices and Subsistence Crises in England and France, 1590–1640', *Journal of Economic History*, xxxix, 1979.

113 Beier, A. L., 'Vagrants and the Social Order in Elizabethan England', *Past and Present*, 64, August 1974.

114 Beier, A. L., Debate on 'Vagrants and the Social Order in Elizabethan England', *Past and Present*, 71, May 1976.

115 Beier, A. L., 'Social problems in Elizabethan London', *Journal of Interdisciplinary History*, ix: 2, 1978–9.

116 Beier, A. L., 'The social problems of an Elizabethan country town: Warwick, 1580–1590' in P. Clark ed., *Country towns in pre-industrial England*, Leicester University Press, 1981.

117 Bittle, W. G. and Lane, R. T., 'Inflation and philanthropy in England: a re-assessment of W. K. Jordan's data', *Economic History Review*, 2nd series, xxix, 1976.

118 Bittle, W. G. and Lane, R. T., 'A Re-Assessment Reiterated', *Economic History Review*, xxxi, 1, 1978.

119 Blanchard, Ian, 'Population Change, Enclosure, and the Early Tudor Economy', *Economic History Review*, 2nd series, xxiii, 3, 1970.

120 Chandler, W. B. H., 'Directions to Overseers of the Poor, 1595', *Norfolk Archaeology*, xxxii (iii), 1960.

121 Clark, P., 'The migrant in Kentish towns, 1580–1640' in P. Clark and P. Slack, eds. *Crisis and Order in English Towns, 1500–1700*, Routledge, 1972.

122 Clark, P., 'Popular Protest and Disturbance in Kent, 1558–1640', *Economic History Review*, xxix, 3, 1976.

123 Clarke, Basil, 'Norfolk Licences to Beg: an unpublished collection', *Norfolk Archaeology*, xxxv, 1972.

124 Coleman, D. C., 'Philanthropy Deflated: A Comment' *Economic History Review*, xxxi, 1, 1978.

125 Dymond, David, 'The Famine of 1527 in Essex', *Local Population Studies*, No. 26, Spring 1981.

126 Gould, J. D., 'Bittle and Lane on Charity: An Uncharitable Comment', *Economic History Review*, xxxi, 1, 1978.

127 Hadwin, J. F., 'Deflating Philanthropy', *Economic History Review*, xxxi, 1, 1978.

128 Harrison, C. J., 'Grain price analysis and harvest qualities, 1465–1634', *Agricultural History Review*, xix, 1971.

129 Kent, Joan R., 'Population Mobility and Alms: Poor migrants in the Midlands during the early seventeenth century', *Local Population Studies*, 27, Autumn 1981.

130 Miskimin, H. A., 'Population growth and the price revolution in England', *Journal of European Economic History*, iv, 1975.

131 Outhwaite, R. B., 'Food crises in early modern England: patterns of public response', *Proceedings of the Seventh International Economic History Congress*, Vol. 2, 1978, ed. M. W. Flinn.

132 Pearson, P. C., 'Elizabethan Poor', *Norfolk Archaeology*, xxxv, 1973.

133 Pound, J. F., Debate on 'Vagrants and the Social Order in Elizabethan England', *Past and Present*, 71, May 1976.

134 Pound, J. F., 'The Validity of the Freemen's Lists: some Norwich evidence', *Economic History Review*, 2nd series, xxxiv, Feb. 1981.

135 Siraut, Mary, 'Physical mobility in Elizabethan Cambridge', *Local Population Studies*, 27, Autumn 1981.

136 Slack, P., 'Poverty and politics in Salisbury, 1597–1666', in P. Clark and P. Slack, eds, *Crisis and Order in English Towns, 1500–1700*, Routledge, 1972.

137 Slack, P., 'Vagrants and vagrancy in England, 1598–1664', *Economic History Review*, 2nd series, xxviii, 1974.

138 Slack, P., 'Books of orders: the making of English social policy, 1577–1631', *Transactions of the Royal Historical Society*, 5th series, xxx, 1980.

139 Slack, P., 'Social Policy and the Constraints of Government, 1547–58' in Jennifer Loach and Robert Tittler, eds *The mid-Tudor Polity, c. 1540–1560*, Macmillan, 1980.

140 Walter, J. and Wrightson, K., 'Dearth and the social order in early modern England', *Past and Present*, 71, 1976.

141 Woodward, D. M., 'The Background to the Statute of Artificers: The Genesis of Labour Policy, 1558–1603', *Economic History Review*, 2nd series, xxxiii, 1980.

142 Woodward, D. M., 'Wage-rates and living standards in pre-industrial England', *Past and Present*, 91, 1981.

143 Zell, Michael, 'Economic Problems of the Parochial Clergy in the Sixteenth Century' in R. O'Day and F. Heal, eds, *Princes and Paupers in the English Church*, Leicester University Press, 1981.

BOOK REVIEWS

143 Coleman, D. C., Review of Jordan's *Philanthropy in England. Economic History Review*, 2nd series xiii, 1960, pp. 113–15.

THESES

144 Hill, J., 'A Study of Poverty and Poor Relief in Shropshire, 1550–1685', Liverpool University MA, 1973.

145 Pound, J. F., 'Government and Society in Tudor and Stuart Norwich', Leicester University PhD, 1974.

ADDENDA

146 Riis, Thomas, ed., *Aspects of Poverty in Early Modern Europe* Alphen aan den Rijn, 1981, containing, *inter alia*, articles by J. F. Hadwin, 'The Problem of Poverty in Early Modern England'; P. A. Slack, 'Comment: Some Comparative Problems in the English Case'; and Charles Wilson, 'Poverty and Philanthropy in Early Modern England'.

147 Herlan, R. W., 'Relief of the Poor in Bristol from late Elizabethan times until the Restoration Era', *Proceedings of the American Philosophical Society*, Vol. 126, No. 3, 1982.

148 Clark, P., ed., *The European Crisis of the 1590s* London, 1985, containing, *inter alia*, articles by P. Clark, 'A Crisis Contained? The Condition of English Towns in the 1590s'; C. S. L. Davies, 'Popular Disorder'; R. B. Outhwaite, 'Dearth, the English Crown and the Crisis of the 1590s'; and D. Souden, 'Demographic Crisis and Europe in the 1590s'.

149 Walter, J., 'A "Rising of the People"? The Oxfordshire Rising of 1596', *Past and Present*, 107, May 1985.

150 Pound, J. F., 'Clerical Poverty in the Early Sixteenth Century: some East Anglian evidence', *Journal of Ecclesiastical History* (forthcoming).

151 Pound, J. F., ed., *Wealth, Poverty and Occupation in Early Modern Suffolk: the Military Survey of 1522 for Babergh Hundred*, Suffolk Records Society, (forthcoming).

Index

Acknowledgements

We are grateful to the following for permission to reproduce copyright material.

George Allen and Unwin for extracts from *Philanthropy in England* by W. K. Jordan; the late Dame Kitty Anderson for extracts from her thesis *The treatment of vagrancy and the relief of the poor and destitute in the Tudor period, based upon the local records of London to 1552 and Hull to 1576*; Edward Arnold Limited for extracts from *Commercial Trends and Policy in Sixteenth Century England* by F. J. Fisher in *Essays in Economic History, Volume I*, edited by E. Carus-Wilson; G. Bell and Sons Limited for an extract from *England under the Yorkists and Tudors* by P. J. Helm and extracts from *English Economic History* by Bland, Brown and Tawney; Cambridge University Press for extracts from *A Discourse of the Common Weal of this Realm of England* by E. Lamond; The Clarendon Press, Oxford for an extract from Sir Thomas More's *Utopia* translated by Robynson and edited by J. C. Collins 1904; The Norfolk and Norwich Joint Records Committee for quotations from original documents in the possession of the Norfolk and Norwich Record Office (in particular for documents 11 and 13) and Routledge and Kegan Paul Limited for extracts from *The Elizabethan Underworld* by A. V. Judges.

Cover: Beggars and tramps, 1509, from the *Shyp of Folys* by Alexander Barclay; photo: Mansell Collection.